THE SOUL CONTRACT

*A Love Story of Forgiveness
and Divine Timing*

ANA WARNER

Published by The Anico Company Nov, 2017
ISBN: 9781775153702

Editor: Danielle Anderson
Typeset: Greg Salisbury
Book Cover Design: Judith Mazari

This book is dedicated to those who dare to dream
and fearlessly bring their dreams to fruition.

Testimonials

Ana is such an amazing storyteller. This book is a fantastic story about the bigger reason(s) for relationships. What a powerful way to share these lessons from grandmother to granddaughter. It is captivating, emotional, raw and provoking story. Once I started I couldn't stop reading it. This book is a must read to help people view their relationship from a new perspective.

Aaron Solly, Best Selling Author, Coach, Counsellor, EngageCoachingGroup.com

This book is destined to teach us important lessons about love! I was drawn into this beautiful love story and it would not let me go. As the story unfolded, I learned about the power of unconditional love. Sometimes love presents itself with life challenges which could result in two people destined to be together, not completing their soul contract. Perhaps the timing is not quite right, the first, second, or third time around, but love will prevail when the divine timing is right! The timing is perfect for "The Soul Contract" because we are here to learn about love!

Dr Luv, R.L.M., Creator of *Syncrohearts* (as seen on Dragon's Den) and Best Selling Author.

Acknowledgements

I would like to express my sincerest gratitude to Julie Salisbury, Founder of Influence Publishing who held my hand and saw me through to the launch of this book. I am also very thankful to Danielle Anderson who provided support, offered comments, and assisted in the editing and proofreading. It has been my absolute pleasure working with you both.

I am also thankful to Cristian Sanchez, whom I have the honor to call my friend, for helping me research the best website options to launch this project.

Above all, I am thankful to God for life, for family and the people whom I have the privilege to call my friends.

Contents

Introduction

I was once told that we are divine souls living in human bodies to experience lessons that help us ascend to a higher spiritual dimension. These experiences come in all forms of relationships which we will encounter during our lifetime, including connections with our family, friends, co-workers and particularly one-on-one love partnerships. As we grow old, these experiences shape our character; we choose to become "good" or "bad" people based on how we react to them. Unfortunately, most of these lessons are painful as they are meant to test our ability to love ourselves unconditionally, and eventually to love others. "Failing" these tests, however, results in a retest (so to speak), either with the same person or with someone else who exhibits the same personality as the individual in our previous affiliation. These lessons lead us to heal ourselves. During the process one can feel entirely alone, as if no one understands the pain and how to move past it. But the truth is, we will all go through the same lessons at one point or another in our lifetime.

While it is true that the people we give our hearts to have the most power to hurt us, they also bring us our greatest lessons of self-love. They give us the choice of learning forgiveness of self and others, a trait that is so difficult to master. Yet once we learn to forgive, we find freedom.

The Buddhist say it best; when the student is ready, the teacher will appear. I hope Malaika's lessons in this book teach you one thing: you are not alone.

Preface

Amal walks through the hallways of The Pike Building, searching for her school counselor's office with her thoughts running rampant. *I can't believe I have to explain myself…oh great, I can't find his office and my appointment starts in four minutes.*

Her phone rings. *Great, it's mom.* She ignores the call and finds room 28. Inside she finds her mother and the school counsellor waiting for her. She turns to the counsellor and says, "Hello, my name is Amal. I have an appointment with you." The counsellor introduces himself, but before he can continue Amal turns to face her mother. "Mom, before you say anything, I didn't attack her; she said some shit I wasn't trying to hear. I told her to back off and she didn't, so I punched her in the throat."

"I don't care, Amal," her mother replies, her voice filled with anger. "You've been expelled for fighting and I've had enough of your bullshit. Your grandmother suggested that you live with her for a little while, and this is exactly what you are going to do."

"You can't force me to move in with grandma! I am my own woman!"

"Your own woman Amal? Do you know how bills are paid? Do you contribute to our household? You don't even clean your room. I have failed you by giving you everything you could ever possibly need and want. You are going to stay with your grandparents for a little while, and that is final.

Maybe my mother can knock some sense into you."

Amal cries during the long drive to Toronto International Airport, and through the entire flight to Vancouver. Upon her arrival, it is raining as usual and her grandparents are waiting for her. "Hello Grandma Malaika and Grandpa Jo! Just so you both know, I am not here by choice." Grandma Malaika smiles and gives Amal a tight hug.

"Amal, welcome," she says warmly. "Now that you are here, we need to set some ground rules. Yes, there are rules in this house. When you step foot outside, you can be wherever you want to be; in this house, though, you are in Malaika's castle and my rules must be followed."

After dinner, Grandma sits down with Amal and asks her why she was so angry. She responds that the girl she knocked unconscious "stole" her man, and that was unacceptable. Amal also vandalized her boyfriend's car for being unfaithful to her and she believes she was right to do this. After all, she is pretty, well-dressed, and a good person, so she does not deserve to be disrespected. Anyone who dares to do so will pay the price. This is how life works, Amal announces, no matter what anyone says.

Grandma Malaika smiles. "Amal, our hearts were meant to be broken so that light can shine in. How people treat us says everything about them, but how we react to such treatment says everything about us. You were wrong to attack that girl, and you were wrong to vandalize your boyfriend's car."

Sobbing, Amal says, "Grandma, I loved him and he said he loved me. How could he? You don't understand, you've never had your heart broken."

"I understand you more than you know, Amal. I too was hot-headed, not just when I was around your age but for majority of my life. The older I have gotten, the calmer I have become because I have learned to see life and people as they are instead of how I want them to be. I also have grown to understand that the only person I could ever control is me and no one else. Once I accepted this fact, I lived with very little stress."

Amal is still weeping. "Stop crying little girl," Malaika admonishes, "I know more of heart break than you think. People come into our lives to teach us lessons and unfortunately, most of the time these lessons are painful. You are young, and the way you handled your breakup says to me that you don't need to be in a relationship right now. Until you understand who you are and how to conduct yourself when things don't go your way, you will continue to attract the same experience until you learn the lesson.

"Your Grandpa Jo and I have had a lot of challenges in our lives, but how we handled them and how we related to each other helped pull us through. He is my best friend, which is how our relationship started; that friendship love is what has helped us when things got tough. Every day with him is a blessing. But it took a long time for me to find stability in my love life; I needed to learn a lot of lessons about love."

Amal dries her tears and lets out a frustrated sigh. "I don't understand, Grandma. How am I supposed to know when I'm ready for a relationship? How do I find a love like you and Grandpa have?"

"Sit with me, Amal," Malaika replies. "I will tell you my story, and your questions will be answered."

❧ Chapter One ❧

"A wise man never knows it all,
only a fool knows everything"
African proverb

Before I married your Grandpa, my name was Malaika Belaweh. I am a second generation African as my parents immigrated to Canada. Our culture here counts success by the number of degrees one has acquired, but I didn't think of degrees; I thought of my purpose, why am I here and how did I end up here. I did fulfil my father's dream to graduate from an accredited University and I received a Bachelor of Science in Biology, but I had no care or desire to become a doctor as my father wanted. Going to medical school was his dream, not mine. I am scared shitless of blood, I don't like the smells of hospitals, and did I mention the sight of blood makes me nauseous?! Also, I am not a damn people person. Being polite doesn't come naturally to me.

I was much more interested in love, photography, and things that are deeper than the eyes can see. As a young

1

girl I thought I had no "luck" in finding that unconditional love that you see in the movies. Yes, yes, I know they are just movies and not real, but I hadn't been loved properly. I had met a few men and deeply cared for them, but I was never *in* love. My life seemed incomplete. I found myself saying and thinking that I was the problem, and I believed that I was the reason that love did not love me. Mind you, I had a pre-conceived notion of what love looked and behaved like. But life was about to teach me otherwise.

I was out of college and living by myself. I made decent money and I had my own home and car, pretty much everything a young woman could need. But all my relationships up to that point had failed, which lead me to believe that I was at fault. Perhaps I was too independent, or perhaps I had limiting beliefs of what love should look like.

I was a late bloomer, I did not have sex until college. My first lover was handsome; I saw him walk in the building during my second year of college and his looks caught my attention. He wasn't exactly the smartest person I had met, but he was attractive and he had a good heart. He dropped out of college the year we met to "find himself" and six years later he still hadn't found what he was looking for. He couldn't hold down a job, which meant he could never afford his rent, so I told him he could move in with me until he found work. That was a bad idea. I lost interest in being the only one with ambition and the only one supporting us. He did not have the courage to find his purpose. His aspirations were so low that he gave up whenever he reached a road block. He never finished what he started, and that for me was the most unattractive thing about him.

He wanted to marry me, although I'm not sure if he loved me or if he loved the fact that I put food on the table and kept a roof over his head. But as time passed, I grew resentful towards him. I couldn't imagine building a life with someone who had no motivation, or feeding a grown man who called in sick more times than he worked. How am I supposed to follow someone who doesn't know where he is going?

I knew I had to end things with him after we went to dinner with both our parents and he brought up marriage... again. My skin broke into hives when everyone got excited talking about it. Little did my family know, I was dealing with a lot of his bullshit and his lack of direction. Later that night, I ended the relationship and asked him to move out of my house. It was difficult but I learned a valuable lesson, although it took some time for me to find out what that was.

At first, I thought my lesson was that some men have no drive; they aim so low that they have nothing to offer intellectually. I wasn't in love with him, that's for sure, but I did love him in my own way. As time passed, however, I began to lose respect for his lack of drive and became irritated by the fact that he had no determination. Life was boring with him. I was stuck in a routine of working to support us as well as dealing with him and his nonsense. His money-making ideas were always stupid, and he aimed so low as well; he thought a thousand dollars was so much cash. He was always talking about ways to make fast money but never kept a steady job. I grew to resent him. I think it was my lack of respect for him that made me angry every time he would call me. I tried to be patient while he "found" himself and even lived with him for two years – unbeknownst to my parents – but after six years I finally gave up.

At that time, I never looked in the mirror at myself; I only looked at what the other person did. Today, because of my life lessons, I have changed that perspective. Now I know that my experiences in that relationship had nothing to do with him, and everything to do with me. I learned that I was brave enough and stable enough to support a grown man, but what I desired was someone to build a life with. That is why he wasn't the right man for me.

Shortly after I broke up with my ambition–challenged boy, I moved on to another person. His name was Jackson. I did love Mr. Jackson, but he was very different from me in many ways. He never showed his emotions – he held in his anger, his pain, his sadness – and on some level I could see right through him and understand his perspective. The problem was he did not understand himself. He broke my heart in a million pieces. After my relationship with Jackson ended, I met my twin flame. That is when I learned what unconditional love was.

I've learned a lot of lessons about love and life, but one thing is for sure: every time love did not love me, I truly believed that my person was out there and the timing of God would bring us together. But first I had to learn to love myself, despite the harsh lessons I learned from my heartbreak.

I can tell, Amal, that you haven't heard of a twin flame. Have patience, my child, and everything will be explained.

❧ Chapter Two ☙

"Tell me whom you love and I'll tell you who you are"
Creole proverb

I met Jackson at a concert and he was so direct, impolite, and forceful in wanting my number. He wasn't exactly the most attractive man I had ever seen, but he was fit and tall and there was something about him that caught my attention and made him sexy. We exchanged numbers and the next day he called me and asked to see me.

It took two weeks for me to see him again, and when I did I was repulsed. He sounded uneducated, looked rough and was just plain rude to say the least. He said silly things and was unbelievably vulgar. He made me uncomfortable with his sexual analogies. Even though I have a trucker's mouth myself, the date ended in about 30 minutes because I just couldn't take his obscenities. I blew him off a few times after that but he wouldn't leave me alone; constantly leaving me messages and calling me "sweetie." As pathetic as I found his forcefulness, I was lonely and I liked the attention.

One hot summer weekend my girls and I were headed out to a club to shake the week's stress away. I invited Jackson as I hadn't seen him since that disaster of a first date. He came a little late, and when he walked in and saw me his face changed. He looked at me as if he had never seen a woman before. He walked up to me and gave me a hug, a tight and long one. When my friends saw us, they giggled and told me that his dick must be huge because he was not cute. Amal, I would apologize for my language, but since you're having sex – although you shouldn't be – you're very much aware of what a dick is.

Shortly after that, we left the club together as I had brought my car and he needed a ride home. We drove around for hours and talked about everything and nothing. I finally dropped him in front of his apartment, and he invited me to come up and watch a movie. I told him "Yes, I love movies, especially the ones at the theater." Then I said goodnight and I drove away.

The next morning I woke up to two missed calls from Jackson. He asked me if I wanted to go to the movies later that evening, and I called him back saying yes.

Jackson was a consultant, working in my city on an eight-month contract. He grew up with very little and he respected the value of a dollar. Once we got past the silly sexual innuendoes, he told me he was a man who wasn't sure of his future. He did not know if he would be successful, and that fear of failing kept him up at night. He seemed to believe his future laid in the hands of the people he worked for. I must say that I did appreciate the fact that he dared to dream; after my last relationship I was happy to be with someone that wanted more for himself, even though he had no clue how to achieve the success that he was striving for.

We watched a movie about monkeys. He talked during the entire movie, mocking me about being African and saying I might have had a pet monkey and here we were watching a movie about them. He was jovial and he made me laugh. Towards the end of the movie, he held my hand and my heart sunk into my stomach. I was surprised and shocked; he made me feel something. I immediately got scared as I now felt vulnerable.

We drove around again after the movie ended, and when he eventually dropped me off in front of my apartment he got out and opened the door for me. I got out of the car, hugged him and said goodnight. As I turned to walk away, he pulled me back and hugged me some more. Then I felt him kiss me on my neck. That kiss sent goosebumps running though my body. He kept hugging me tightly and eventually his lips made their way to mine. They were soft and full. My heart was racing as we embraced but I had to let go. I was afraid that I would invite him in, and that would bring another kind of trouble…if you know what I mean.

I got into my apartment and could not believe what was happening. All through the night, thoughts were running through my head. *This man is not my type. Why the fuck do I want to take my clothes off and make love to him?*

I finally fell asleep for a few hours, and when I woke up the next morning I found myself hoping he called. And he had. He wished me a good day at work and asked me to call him when I got off.

All day, I could not stop thinking about him. I was almost mad at the fact that I was now interested in his dick game. I called my friend, Neka, and told her what had happened. Her response was exactly what I thought it would be. "Go get a wax and suck his dick, girl. You're single; get some of that thug flavor inside you."

Neka was my ride or die, my right arm, my friend, my confidante, my homie. She was a free-spirited soul who enjoyed life to the fullest. She and I found a bond in listening to old school music, dancing and reminiscing about the times life seemed simple. Neka and I met in third grade; we were the only two black girls in our school, and that pulled us together for life. She was a bit wild and we got into a lot of trouble, but we stuck together through it all. She was the sister I never had, and with her being an only child it's safe to say she loved me as much as I loved her. She was more than a friend; she was family.

Jackson and I started to talk every day and do the kind of stuff couples did, although we weren't in a relationship. We went to dinners and for grocery shopping and took long walks. About a month after we met, we went to a club and danced all night. I had more fun in that one night then I had in a very long time. Prior to that night, I had been in limbo and I was waiting to be happy. Then Jackson came along and I was finally living.

After the all-night clubbing, we walked to his building which was a couple of blocks away. We went into his apartment, made peanut butter and jelly sandwiches and talked. I laughed at his silly and vulgar jokes. By 4:00 a.m. I was beat and he insisted that we cuddle and sleep. I took a shower, put on a t-shirt of his and laid next to him. It felt so good being next to a man that muscular and strong. He held me tight and, of course, we kissed. I felt my heart beating faster and all I wanted to do was make love to him. And so we did. He laid on top of me and kissed me so softly. His hands intertwined with mine the entire time we made love. We held each other after and it felt so good. I got that feeling of comfort and safety that I had never felt before, and it scared me. I got up around 6:00 a.m. and left. He asked me to stay but I couldn't show him that I was feeling something for him, so I rushed to my car and sped off.

I got home and was disappointed in myself. *What the fuck was I doing? Am I falling for him? But he's not my type. He's not ideal for me.* All these thoughts kept running through my mind as I tried to sleep.

I had just finally fallen asleep when he called. I answered and he said, "I wish I had woken up next to you this morning. When can I see you again?"

Something inside of me lit up, but I knew we needed to set rules. I saw him a few days after that and I told him that I wasn't sure what I was doing and where all this was taking us. He said he understood and that he liked me and wanted to spend time with me. He reassured me that eventually we would figure all this out.

As the summer went by, we spent a lot of time together

and we did things he had never done before. I introduced him to the traditional African cuisine my mom cooked and we talked about where we both came from. He taught me how to ride a motorcycle and how to shoot a gun at the range. We went bowling and swimming and we rode jet skis all summer long. Most importantly, I started to love him and I knew he was falling for me too.

When I got a promotion at work, Jackson was so happy for me. He wasn't intimidated by a woman who made more money than he did, and he celebrated my wins as if they were his. He respected my hustle and the fact that I did not wait on any man to feed me. Instead I chose men simply out of what my heart felt. He made enough money, but he had a lot of responsibilities. He helped his family as his father was ill, which made me even more attracted to him. He would say he was perfectly comfortable when I occasionally paid for our dates, although he would buy me flowers the day after. I guess he wanted to even out the spending.

We went to the beach on a hot Sunday afternoon, and that's where we had our first fight. He said something insensitive and I lost my shit. I cussed him the hell out and he laughed which made me even angrier. I insisted he dropped me off at home and I got out of his car and slammed the door while continuing to scream and cuss at him. I told you I have a foul mouth!

He called for two days while I ignored him. Eventually I gave in and we made up. This continued all summer long and into the fall. We loved and hated each other; getting into big fights and then making up.

We did not discuss what our relationship status was. Often I wondered if we were friends with benefits, or was he my boyfriend and I his girlfriend? A part of me did not want to bring up the conversation. I was afraid that he would run away, or that he would fear commitment. I also wasn't sure if I wanted commitment. This was my first mistake with Jackson: I wasn't clear within myself about what I desired from him. That grey area in my expectations caused me a lot of heartache.

Later that week Neka was hosting a party at The Basement, a club we frequently danced at. Neka was a club promoter and knew of all the fun stuff happening in our city.

I got to the club and it was amazing, packed with people I knew and people I would vibe with. Jackson had arrived before me and called me asking where I was. I walked around the two-story establishment looking for him, and I found him talking to another woman. He saw me and smiled, but he wasn't smiling at me with happiness. He was smiling as if to make me jealous. It worked; I immediately turned around and walked out of the club, raced out to my car and left. Neka tried to stop me but I was so angry at the sight of him talking to another woman that I had to leave.

He did not call me that night, or the next day. I was hurt and cried a little, but mostly I was angry.

After four days he called to say hello, and that's all I needed to tell him to go the fuck to hell. I lost my shit and told him to never call me or contact me again. He drove to my house so we could talk in person, and when he arrived we screamed at each other. I cried and cussed at him and asked him to leave. He kept saying he did not know what he did wrong; after all, he could talk to whoever he chose as he wasn't my man. Although he was right, him saying that angered me even more. After I kicked him out of my house we stopped speaking for eleven days, and those days were difficult for me. But I am stubborn and I felt like the victim so I did not reach out. He needed to contact me and apologize, and he needed to take back all the mean shit he said to me.

After eleven days, he called and asked if he could come by to see me. He came with his eyes red and told me that his father's illness was worsening and he needed to head back home. I immediately felt tears in my eyes and a knot in my throat; I didn't want him to leave.

In the days following I helped him pack and move out of his apartment and ran errands for him; it was important for me to keep busy in order to stop myself from crying. The night before he left we did not have sex, we just held each other tightly. That night, I realized he loved me. I watched him go through security at the airport, and it felt like a piece of me was leaving. After he was no longer in sight, I headed to my apartment and to a life without him. I did not know if he would call me when he got home, or if we would ever see each other again. I cried myself to sleep that night; little did I know, that was the beginning of many sleepless, tear-filled nights.

ঙ Chapter Three ৯

"Speak your truth even if your voice shakes"
Unknown

Before Jackson left, I was afraid to define my relationship with him. They say hindsight is 20/20, and today I see that my insecurities and fear about asking for what I wanted is why I hesitated to have "the talk" with him. I was afraid to lose him, but truth is I never had him to begin with.

Two days after Jackson left, he called me. The surprise in my voice when he called irritated him. He said to me, "Malaika, did you think I would not call you? You thought I was going to fly away and never see you again? We need a plan to see each other soon. Can you move to Chicago?"

I was so surprised at the fact that he wanted me to move to his home town and meet his family. I thought he saw me as a summer fling and nothing more. I was happy and scared that we were continuing this "relationship;"

happy because I knew I loved him, and scared because I would have to pack up my life and leave all that is familiar to me if this worked out between us.

Before I moved, though, I wanted us to talk more and be in an actual relationship, even if it was long distance. I wanted to know what I was about to get myself into. So that's what we did, talk! We talked for two months before we finally saw each other again.

The night before I flew to Chicago to see him for the first time was difficult. I couldn't sleep; I was excited, nervous, and anxious at the same time. Neka helped me pick out a sexy ensemble for a surprise I had planned. It was a stripper's outfit, and that thing stung so much; I got a new-found respect for anyone who can wear something digging into their vagina while sliding down a poll.

It took me five hours of travel time to get to Chi-town, plus a taxi ride to our hotel. He couldn't pick me up from the airport as he had to put in a few hours at work that day. He had booked a room in a swanky five-star hotel with a beautiful view of the city. I checked in, took a shower and laid in bed waiting for his arrival.

While I impatiently waited for him, my stomach turned. I wasn't sure what our reactions would be when we saw each other. Then the door handle turned and there he was. I jumped into his arms and hugged him so tightly. He held me and kept saying, "Here's my baby." He lifted me up and I wrapped my legs around his waist as he kissed my lips. He laid me on the bed and we made love.

We spent four days sight-seeing and looking at houses

we jokingly picked out for him to someday buy for me. We checked out the local markets, restaurants, and comedy clubs. The truth is, it didn't matter where he took me; I loved every minute of it. We were together, and in that moment nothing else mattered.

The night before I headed home, I cried as I knew it would be a few months before we saw each other again. He laughed at me while I was crying like a baby, but I knew his laughter was just a deflection from the fact that his eyes were welling up as well. With our commitments to work and family we did not know when we would see each other, and as much as we wanted our relationship to go in a certain direction, our future was uncertain.

I hate goodbyes, Amal, more than anything in this world. I would gladly live with hemorrhoids rather than have to go through the emotions of saying goodbye to someone I love. This goodbye, however, felt a little different. I couldn't tell if I was so emotional because I knew I would miss him, or because I knew in my heart that something was off.

During our relationship there were a lot of things I turned a blind eye to. It was easier for me to live in the few happy moments than to see the bigger picture. There was also something inside of me which kept reminding me that I had unfinished business with him. I wasn't sure what that business was, but I knew I had to see it through.

When I returned home I cried for a week straight. I missed him, and I missed my time with him. I felt lonely even when I was in a room full of people. All I could think of was him, and each time we spoke I felt like he brought me back to life. I loved him, or at least I thought so at the time. Now I realize that we had karma to complete with each other. God sent him in my life to teach me things; about loving myself, and about what it is I desired and deserved.

Now, you may wonder how you can have karma to complete with someone you barely know. Well, I am speaking of karma from a past life. You see Amal, I find it hard to believe that things happen by coincidence. I question how it is possible to meet certain people and love them immediately while other people you meet repulse you. I think some experiences were predestined to come into our lives so that we feel pain that is deeper than anything we imagined possible; hurt that is so bad, it tears our hearts apart and breaks us down completely. But these experiences are what help us to grow in love with ourselves. These hurts allow us to step up the spiritual ladder and enables us to wake up from the limited beliefs we have regarding love and what we deserve. They open our eyes to see how beautiful we are and how strong we can become.

When I returned to Vancouver, Jackson and I started to argue a lot over nothing. He did not like the way I would say things, which made him defensive, and I did not like his responses to my questions, which made me angry. Sometimes I think he would start an argument just to hurt me. We fought and made up and fought some more only to forgive each other once again.

The Christmas party at my firm was around the corner and I had invited him to come along with me. He flew in two days prior and stayed for a week. When he arrived through customs, though, his energy had changed. We hugged and kissed, and I could see in his eyes that he missed me as much as I missed him, but something was off and I did not know what it was. I thought perhaps it was the fact that we hadn't seen each other in a few months and all we did was argue when we talked.

We went back to my apartment, and while he took a shower I called Neka. I told her that Jackson was here, but something was wrong. She jokingly asked me if his "dick was soft." I giggled and told her he seemed sad, as if he was hiding something. She responded by saying, "Your instincts won't lead you astray, follow them."

We walked into my company's Christmas party a few days later, looking like man and wife. My dress matched his tux and he smelled so good. We mingled with my co-workers and laughed the night away, but there was still something about his energy I couldn't explain.

We got home from the party and laid in bed staring at each other. I could sense there were so many things he wanted to say; I could also sense that he loved me. We made plans to see each other again in his hometown in two months as he wanted me to meet his family.

Jackson left, and this time I did not shed a tear. I could feel myself pulling away because I sensed something was off with him, and whatever it was I knew it would affect me. After he left, the ups and downs continued. When things were good, they were really good; when things were bad, they were really bad.

I went out with Neka and her friend Renu one night. This was my first time meeting Renu and she was very cool. She was a little shy, highly educated, and very spiritual. She kept talking about "energies" and I found her view on life to be a breath of fresh air. Renu grew up with a mom who was psychic, read tarot cards and did palm readings. As she shared her experiences with the readings her mom did, I found myself wanting to have one myself. After all, I couldn't shake the feeling that something was wrong with Jackson and I needed answers as he wasn't giving me any.

I walked into Renu's house to get my first ever card reading from her mother. I was nervous yet excited. I wasn't sure what to expect, but I sensed that after this meeting I wouldn't be the same person. Renu's mother came down to the kitchen where I sat and my first impression was that she was so beautiful. She was dressed in her traditional lehenga and she smelled of incense. "Hello Malaika," she said, "my name is Anarta, but you can call me Aunty." I smiled and sat down. Anarta continued, "Card reading predictions are not set in stone, it simply tells us the energy we are currently living with. These energies can change by adjusting our thought patterns as well as the direction we are currently headed in. We all have intuition, and learning to meditate enables us to connect to our higher selves. Learn to slow down and listen to yourself. Don't be afraid to face truths; pleasant or not, face them."

She read my cards and told me Jackson was a soul mate. Meeting him was not a coincidence as I had a "soul contract" with him. She said he was brought into my life to teach me

19

lessons, as I am to teach him about love, and the decisions we both make will determine how easy or how difficult our journey will be together. The choice was in both our hands.

I left that reading a changed person, and I had discovered a new obsession. I wanted to learn everything I could about this new-found topic of spirituality and mediation. I went out in search of knowledge.

The more I meditated and studied myself and my habits, the more I felt like I could express myself without being judged by my family and friends. I know I am a little crazy. I also feel things very deeply, more than others do, and the love I felt for Jackson was real – even if he didn't feel as deeply as I did.

I visited Jackson, and this time we stayed with his parents in their summer home near the lake. His mother wasn't exactly welcoming at first, but after the weekend passed we became friends. We called each other frequently, and she talked to me about her struggles when she was a young woman. Her insights and her life story were so interesting. Her potty mouth was also a breath of fresh air. Boy, could she cuss out a motherfucker if they crossed her! I found her so funny. She was a good woman; she spoke her truth, and she was always to the point.

Another year had come and gone and Jackson and I were doing this back and forth, highs and lows with no end to this long-distance love story in sight. We constantly argued about our future as he wanted me to pack up and move to be with him, and I wanted to be his wife before I did so. After all, I was the one with the stable paycheck and

I did not have a work visa. At least, those were the reasons I gave him; truth is, something inside of me, my intuition, knew he was hiding something. Deep down I also knew that our love affair would not last a life time, but admitting this to myself was not an option. No matter how much he hurt me with his words, I forgave him. No matter how much he disappointed me, I always took him back. I found myself crying almost every night, but I still couldn't walk away from him.

The more difficult things got with Jackson, the more I became obsessed with what made people act the way they do. I read books on astrology, individual natal charts and the psychology of people. I analyzed myself first, of course, and I faced the good things about myself and became conscious of the things that weren't so good. Once I began to see who I was and what was good for me, I pulled away from a lot of "friends" who weren't spiritually aware. My days of aimless hangouts and meaningless conversations were over. I no longer had the energy to deal with people who weren't "awake." I knew I was evolving as a human, and as such I became conscious of the way I treated myself and others. Yet I still couldn't let go of Jackson. I was given so many reasons to move on from this man, and I received the signs from God that I prayed for, but still I couldn't leave him.

As time passed, my relationship with Jackson got worse. We would have one good day and seven bad ones, and he started to accuse me of being unfaithful. On one of his visits, we attended a friend's birthday party. The music was amazing and the crowd was just right. The vibe was exactly what I needed. I went and hugged the birthday boy, and he joked around about how my dress was mighty fitted while complimenting Jackson on being the one who could snatch me. About an hour into the party, Jackson decided to approach the birthday boy and question him about his relationship with me. Apparently the hug was inappropriate in Jackson's eyes. The birthday boy did not seem to like being questioned, and next thing I know punches were being thrown. I was humiliated; these people were my friends and I could not believe Jackson would cause such a commotion. He was never violent, and this side of him wasn't something I would put up with. We were both kicked out of the party and I insisted Jackson changed his flight and leave the next day. We broke up that night, only to make up again a week after he left.

Just when I thought things couldn't get worse, they did. Jackson wanted to know my every move. When I went out with my friends, he wanted to know the address of the restaurant or event I was attending, as if he intended on sending the police to spy on me and report back to him. We were both on the defensive, and every time I would see his number show up on my caller ID I instantly got a migraine. We would constantly break up and make up. Each day that went by I grew angrier, and I directed that anger towards everyone but him.

We had a fight so bad once that we decided to see each other in person to discuss it. Making up on the phone was not going to help this time, so I flew to Chicago to see him. When I arrived, his energy was one of fear – it's like I could sense he was afraid that this visit would be the last and that this would be the final time he saw me. He held on to me so tightly, and he would follow me around as if I would run away if he wasn't watching. When I asked him what was wrong he answered that he missed me and was happy to see me, but that little voice in my head kept telling me he was lying. There was more to this than I knew.

During the visit I asked if we could see his family; his mom and I had become very good friends and I wanted to visit her. She had a way of making me laugh. Every time she saw me she chanted the same song: "Oh, there's my future daughter-in-law and bitch is giving me body. That booty can buy you a Murciélago girl. What you doing with my broke-ass son?" He told me his family was out of town so we couldn't see them.

A few days later I left on the red eye back to Vancouver, and this time everything inside me knew that this would be the last time I would ever see him. I don't know how or why I felt this way because the visit was good. He dropped me off at the airport and walked me to security; we hugged, and we both knew that things would never be the same after I got on that flight. For the first time since I met Jackson I saw tears run down his face, and my eyes watered as well. We held each other tightly and kissed softly. He caressed my hair and back and he wouldn't let go. I walked through security, and he stood watching me until I was no longer in sight. I loved him with everything inside me; I loved him more than I had ever loved any man prior to him. But I knew that day that I would never see him again.

The next morning I arrived late to work, jetlagged and hungry, and had a ton of work to do. I took a bite into my bagel and cream cheese and my phone rang. It was Jackson's mom. Strange that she was calling early this morning. I answered, and this time her voice was different.

After the usual pleasantries, she told me, "When I met you, Malaika, I wasn't sure what to think of you. You are so beautiful and highly educated and you could get any man you wanted, yet you choose my son who had nothing to offer you. I see you love that boy, more than he deserves, and because of that I grew to love you too."

As she continued to speak, I could feel my heart beating and I began to panic. "Mama Jackson, are you okay? Is Jackson okay?" She sighed and said "Yes, Jackson is fine and so am I. But I need to tell you something. I was hoping to tell you in person, but you did not come to see me when you were here this past weekend." Surprised, I told her that Jackson said she was out of town. "No, Malaika, we were here and I needed to see you. I'm so sorry that I have to be the one to tell you this, but I love you like a daughter and the longer Jackson delays telling you the worse I believe it will be. Jackson fathered a child with a woman he barely knows. The kid is fourteen months old, and the DNA don't lie – the child is his, and he is going to take care of that child if it's the last thing I make him do. I thought you should know this before you move your life here. You deserve to know the truth, and I'm sorry my son isn't man enough to tell you himself."

I instantly felt light headed, and all I could manage to

say was, "Thank you for calling me Mama Jackson, I am at work and I need to go."

I hung up the phone and my blood rushed to my feet. I felt dizzy even though I was sitting down. I called Jackson's phone and when he answered I calmly asked him, "Jackson, do you have a child?" His response was priceless; he started screaming and cussing. I said nothing else and hung up the phone. I immediately asked IT to block his calls to my direct line. I grabbed my hand bag, went into my boss' office and told him I had a family emergency and needed to leave. I went directly to a walk-in clinic and asked for a screening for every STD known to man. I sat through the humiliation of a doctor lecturing me about unprotected sex; I wasn't the promiscuous one, yet I was being treated like I was.

I then drove to a lake about two hours outside of the city. I walked the shoreline and cried, screamed, felt every emotion I needed to feel. I was angry, mostly at myself. I knew Jackson wasn't the man for me, yet I was willing to settle for someone who was no good. I thought I could love him until he loved himself. I then understood that he couldn't give me what he did not have; he did not love himself enough to love me. I held myself responsible for my own feelings because I never held anyone responsible for my experiences; good or bad, they are still mine.

I spent all day by the water, and all I could feel was anger. I checked my phone messages and saw that Jackson had left me fourteen messages, so I called my phone company and had his number blocked. This was the end.

I had nothing more to say and I did not need him to find closure. Instead, I needed to find forgiveness and closure within myself.

All kinds of thoughts ran through my head that day, mostly negative thoughts about myself. How could I be so stupid? I was humiliated, hurt and betrayed by the closest person to me. I had to acknowledge that as I was fighting for this relationship to work, in reality I was fighting to be lied to, cheated on and taken for granted; fighting to be hurt, disappointed and betrayed by someone I envisioned spending the rest of my life with. It was my fault because, in my heart, I knew better. I knew this was never going to work out, but I kept fighting for him to love me the way I deserved to be loved.

I then remembered my visit to the psychic, Aunty Anarta. Was she right? And if so, what was the lesson I needed to learn? Was I wrong for loving someone? Why is God punishing me for caring about another person? What did I do so wrong to deserve this?

I only told Neka what had happened, and no one else. I was too embarrassed. I did not dare tell my parents because I knew they would judge me. Everything in my apartment reminded me of Jackson, so Neka said I could stay with her for a while so I wasn't alone. She was like my sister, and it sure did help me to talk to her.

A few days after I received this new-found information, I got a call from my high-rise security saying Jackson was in the lobby and wanted to go up to my suite. I asked them not to let him in. He had flown five hours to talk to me, but he never made that sort of effort when we were together. I called his mother and asked her to tell him to leave, because if he didn't I would call the police. I wanted nothing to do with him, and I sure as hell did not want to talk to him.

A few weeks later, I moved because I needed a fresh start and to get away from all the reminders of him. For weeks and months after I moved, though, I still cried myself to sleep every night. I stopped all communication with him and his family. I did not want to hear his voice or see him. I hated him. I knew I needed to forgive Jackson to set myself free and make myself happy again, but I couldn't do it. Today, I understand that Jackson passed through my life in a shorter time frame than I had hoped to teach me things he never could have taught me if he stayed.

The lesson was about self-love, but at the time I still did not learn it. So, life was about to teach me the same lesson again.

❧ Chapter Four ❧

"The heart was made to be broken"
Oscar Wilde

Two years had come and gone but my heartache persisted. I became afraid to open up to people – afraid to let people in. I was always on the defensive and protecting myself without realizing that this was the energy I was projecting. I spent my free time on the tracks, running. I also read books; books about self-healing, books on forgiveness – especially self-forgiveness – and books regarding God.

I spent every Sunday in church because it gave me a sense of peace. I found gratitude knowing that the Almighty God loved me despite my shortcomings. I learned to meditate and to listen to my intuition. The more I listened to that little voice we tend to ignore, the more I grew to see right through people. I noticed every little thing about someone without even trying; it seemed like I could tell what they were thinking. The truth is, people always show us who they are as long as we pay attention, and I paid close attention.

During this time I was not only single, but also celibate as well. I had not been on a date or met anyone of interest. Loneliness crept in, but I was adamant to only give my energy to someone I saw a future with.

Neka was hosting a party on the rooftop of a hotel, and this was the first time I had been out in a very long time. I wore jeans and a tank top with heels as I was in no mood to dress up. My makeup was light; I looked like I was going grocery shopping. The party was amazing, the music was great and there was a lot of fantastic people.

Then in came a handsome man – and I do mean handsome. I immediately got shy when he looked my way and smiled. He walked towards me and asked me to dance, then held my hand and led me to the dance floor. As we got in the middle of the floor, the DJ switched his tune to none other than Diana King's "Shy Guy." That made things interesting to say the least. He held me close and we danced like we were making love. It felt good to have a man hold me so firmly, and he smelled so good. He whispered softly in my ear, "I meant to introduce myself. My name is Cameron, what's yours?" I smiled and responded, "Malaika." "That's a unique name. I love it, and so would my mom." I awkwardly smiled as I wasn't sure how to take him talking about his mom with me, a total stranger. But something about him and the way he conducted himself that night said he was looking for a committed relationship. We exchanged numbers and later that night – well more like around 4:00 a.m. when the party was over – he called me to say it was a pleasure meeting me and to wish me goodnight.

Several days later, Cameron called me and asked me out on a proper date. It had been so long since I dated someone, I wasn't sure how to act. I was a little nervous but I was happy to spend a Sunday afternoon with a nice man. Plus, let me reiterate, he was incredibly handsome.

When Cameron arrived, he greeted me with, "Hey there, sorry I am late. I am on colored-people time." I smiled and we began our walk by the ocean. He told me about his family, showed me pictures and talked about his hobbies. When we stopped to eat, I asked the tough question. "So, Cameron, why am I here? What are you looking for?" He responded, "I am looking for a relationship. I like you, your energy is chill and I want to get to know you better." I nodded and changed the subject. We walked some more after dinner and talked about our life goals. I liked him; he was attractive, and he had his life figured out. But the more we walked and talked, the more I couldn't help but feel that he wasn't "the one." He said all the right things and he was a proper gentleman, but something was missing and I wasn't sure what that was.

After our date, he dropped me off at home and kissed me. I felt absolutely nothing from that kiss; there was zero chemistry between us. I went home after our date and Cameron did not cross my mind, and that was not a good sign. Instead, I sat on my couch and day-dreamed of what my husband would be like.

The next morning Cameron called while I was getting ready for work and asked me out to a movie later that week. I told him I'd call him back at noon but got caught up with running errands for my mom. Later that night, he called again while he was out drinking with his buddies. "Who drinks on a Monday night," I mumbled to myself after we got off the phone. That was also a sign that Cameron and I were not compatible. I socially drank, but going for drinks on a Monday night would not be something I would ever do.

We hung out once again, and I knew that I needed to tell him that I wasn't feeling any connection. I did not want to string him along, nor did I want to hurt him. The sooner I let him know, the better. It was unfair to stay with him when I was wishing he was someone else. I wasn't sure who I wanted him to be, but I knew it wasn't him; he wasn't right for me. My person was out there, and he was on his way to find me. Whoever he was, I knew that I would know him once he arrived in my life. He would turn my life upside down and stir things in my heart and soul that I did not know was possible, and I was willing to wait for him.

A few days later I called Cameron and told him I wasn't feeling a connection. He sounded very disappointed and a bit mad. He said I could have taken more time to get to know him, but deep down I couldn't lead him on knowing I did not see a future with him. That call broke my heart.

I also hated that I wasn't going to accompany him to his friend Amie's party. I met Amie through Cameron and we clicked immediately. When I did not show up with Cameron to her party she insisted that he give her my number, and when he finally did she left me a message. I called her and we went out and did girly things. It was nice to meet someone I connected with; as much as I loved Neka, her schedule was different from mine and I barely saw her. Amie lived and worked closer to me and she eventually became a good friend. It was great having someone to laugh with and talk trash with, and her mouth was just as foul as mine; yes, she was one of my soulmates.

Amie had a tough life. She did not have the most loving family, but she found her way. She made some mistakes and wasn't afraid to speak of them. She, like me, had been unlucky in love, but she was hopeful. However, her actions with the men in her life did not exactly reflect her wanting a long-term partner to share her life with. She was very promiscuous, though I never judged her.

Amie quickly became my confidant, and I became hers. We talked about everything and laughed about the things we couldn't change. I did not trust anyone but Neka; however, Amie seemed to be on the road of becoming a great friend.

Cameron wasn't happy that "his friend" and I were hanging out; he still believed that we should be together. The truth, though, is that I was still heartbroken over my experience with Jackson, and even if there was chemistry between us my hurt wouldn't allow me to trust Cameron's intentions. My lack of trust had nothing to do with him and everything to do with me. I did not have the heart to drag him into my pain which had yet to heal; the last thing I wanted was to hurt him. I couldn't be one of those women who would date someone while having one foot out the door. Stringing him along would only destroy his perspective on love, and I couldn't be responsible for that.

❧ Chapter Five ❧

"Love, like rain, does not choose the grass
on which it falls"
African proverb

We planned a girl's trip to Vegas for my birthday, but Neka
got a DUI and had to appear in court. I did not want to go
anywhere without my girl so I chose to go to dinner and a
club in Vancouver instead. The girls came out to help me
celebrate, and it was the best time I'd had in years. While at
dinner, it became time to blow out my candles and make a
wish. I wished for a good man; someone to build a life with,
someone who makes my heart skip a beat. I prayed for God
to send me my life partner.

We left dinner and arrived at the club. There was lineup
but Neka of course knew the bouncer so he allowed us to
skip through the lineup and head into the club. I walked in
and there he was. The one. My person. My twin flame.

He was handsome, tall, dark-skinned and he had the
biggest smile I had ever seen. By the way he dressed, it was

clear he was not from around here. Our eyes locked and he stared at me while I walked towards him. He smiled and said, "Hello, do you live in Vancouver? I've never seen you in this place before." I looked in his eyes and knew I already loved him.

I know, Amal, it sounds crazy, but he was familiar; he felt like an old friend. I knew him even though we had never met. I knew what he was thinking without him having to say it. I also knew I was in love with him.

We talked to each other – well, more like yelled over the music – and we exchanged numbers. Later that night, after we left the club, he called me and asked me to dinner the next day.

I couldn't sleep that night. I found myself thinking about this man. His name was Elijah Monroe, or Eli as he preferred to be called. We went on our first date the following day, which ended up lasting for two days. Yes he stayed with me, and no we did not have sex. We talked and laughed and went for walks and out to dinner. It felt as if he was someone I had known my whole life. He was my missing piece. I was open for the first time in years; I wanted to get to know him, and I wanted him to know me. We cuddled in bed and talked some more. He made me laugh and boy, did he like to talk. We had similar interests and we wanted the same things in this life.

After that weekend, we were inseparable; we talked all day long. We saw each other at night and we had the best conversations. I was so comfortable around him. We cooked for each other and shared our deepest fears and greatest desires. I was in love with him and he was in love with me. I could see his soul, and he could see mine. This was my person, my twin flame. He was the one.

One night we sat on his bed, listening to the rain beat against his apartment window. We laid in silence and then he pulled my face towards his and said, "Malaika, I have never met anyone like you before. I have never felt this strong pull towards someone. You're my weakness." That night, we made love for the first time. I can't describe what that was like; for the first time in my life, I truly felt love. My heart was reawakened.

We spent a few more weeks falling in love, but soon Christmas arrived and Eli was heading home for the holidays. As sad as I was that he was leaving, I couldn't wait till he returned. He was gone for three weeks, and when it was finally time for him to come back I woke up so happy. I counted down the hours until his flight arrived, and I was so excited to see him that I got to the airport two hours early. But when he returned, something had changed.

Eli and I had a good thing going, until he went to visit his family. I now know that he told his family about me and they did not approve of me. I am a black girl of African descent, but I am North American. The only thing African about me are my parents. Although he is also a black man, he was adopted by an African family when his biological parents died in a car crash. This family were great friends of his parents, and they have raised him and his older brother since he was five. He grew up in England with a strong emphasis on his African culture. I admired that about him since I did not know much about my own African heritage. I preferred pizza for dinner as opposed to fufu and groundnut soup. He was a strict Christian and I liked my wine. I knew right from wrong, but I was by no means traditional.

His only reason for being in Vancouver was to complete his studies. The plan was for him to graduate with an undergraduate degree and then receive his masters as well. After that, it was back to England to live a traditional life, including being married to a "real" African girl his mother approved of. There was nothing about a girl like myself that fell into the perfectly planned life his family envisioned for him.

So, when he came back from his trip to visit his family, everything changed between us. He started to mistreat me and I did not understand why. He wanted me around, and then he didn't. He would come to see me and then leave shortly after. The most painful part was when he stopped looking directly into my eyes.

He became annoying as well. He would call me at all hours of the night, and when I would answer he would apologize and claim he didn't have anything to say. There were times where I was convinced he was bipolar or high on something. His behavior became so strange, he was like a completely different person.

I did not understand what the fuck was going on. After a few weeks of that shit, I called him and told him that I needed to talk to him and I was coming over to his home. I arrived there and I could see he was sad; I asked what was wrong and he didn't respond. In fact, he quickly got annoyed with my question. I asked him what his problem was, but I wasn't ready for his response.

He told me that he would never marry me, and if he had given me any mixed signals about wanting a relationship with me he was now correcting that. He did not want to see me or be with me, he had no tolerance for someone so different like me. He was abrupt and he seemed angry at me, although I had done nothing to deserve it.

To say I was shocked and speechless after what he said would be an understatement. All I could do was say "okay" and leave.

I drove away, unable to comprehend what had just happened. I was angry and confused at the same time. I called Neka, and when she picked up I said, "Bitch you ain't gonna believe what this fool just told me." After I explained what had just happened, she angrily said, "The fuck did that muthafucker say? He must not know about you. This bitch just insulted you and you calling me to tell me you did not shoot him or at the least run him over?"

I did not sleep for two days after that bullshit. I was angry and hurt, but mostly confused.

A week went by and Eli finally called me asking if we could talk. We met up and he wanted to pretend like nothing happened. He spoke to me as if we were on friendly terms. I, of course, don't sweep things under the rug, so I cut him off while he was making small talk and questioned his behavior. He said I was sensitive and he just talks foolishness and did not mean what he said. I accepted his apology, but my guard went up.

This was just the beginning of the five years of madness that followed.

A week after that fight, Eli invited me to see his new apartment. It was cozy and comfortable, and I felt at home at his place. Perhaps it was the warmth I felt every time he held me close. As hesitant as I was about what had transpired, I decided to give our relationship another shot.

During my visit, we made mac and cheese from the box, sat on the rug and ate it; this became a tradition for us. We played like siblings, we talked like best friends, we fought like husband and wife, and as time went by I realized that this relationship was different. I had loved hard before meeting Eli, but for the first time I understood what it was like to truly love someone unconditionally. He, however, did not love me in return. This is because he feared the connection between us, and he thought it was too good to be true; at least, that's what he told me every time he mistreated me.

As time went on, Eli's games escalated. He would make plans with me and not show up. He would call me and apologize, but then do the same thing again. When I would cut him off, he would try even harder to get me to talk to him. We would argue about our cultural and religious differences and stop speaking for weeks. Then he would return to my life to start it all over again.

Every time we fought we would have makeup sex and that "fixed" things between us. I loved him, and I wanted to show him this by sharing my body with him. We were comfortable enough to talk about our sexual likes and dislikes, favorite positions, anything and everything. I was never once uncomfortable telling this man my deepest desires, and he told me his. We both listened to each other without judgment. The sexual attraction between us was so intense that I sometimes feared that it was all we had.

The more we hung out, the more I fell for him. He was funny, smart, literate, and he could whip up a meal like a gourmet chef. Basically, he was the male version of me, except he was much better at cooking. However, we were also very different. We wanted the same things out of life but had our own methods of pursuing those desires. The more I listened to his reasonings, the more I loved him and the more my mind expanded. The same was true for him; he once told me that listening to me speak of my views on life had provoked him to think about the meaning of his own life and what his purpose was on this planet.

The deeper we connected, the more Eli would run away without a word. He would stop calling me for weeks and then suddenly reappear. I wasn't sure why this was happening, and whenever I questioned him he would apologize and say he had some family issues he needed to take care of. When I asked what those "issues" were, he would change the subject. I knew he was hiding something, and as I had learned from my lessons with Jackson, I paid attention to my intuition. Since Eli didn't want to tell me what was really going on, I had to protect myself.

I stopped having sex with him. I would only meet in public places, and when he would ask why I was changing I played dumb. Although I had temporarily "friendzoned" him until I found out the truth, I kept falling more and more in love with him.

One afternoon Neka had called me over to her house for some girl talk, and what she was about to tell me broke my heart in a million pieces.

Neka had run into Eli during his latest disappearance, and he was not alone. Eli was with his mother and his fiancée. Yes, his mother made sure to let Neka know that the woman sitting with them was his fiancée, who he had known since childhood and who was the only woman she would ever approve of. This woman was that girl who cooked the fufu and groundnut soup, the one who would graduate from college and be a good wife to her son.

I cried and cried, and then I got angry. I called Eli and he didn't answer so, being the hot-head that I was, I went over to his house. Good thing that I saw him pull into the gas station by his apartment before reaching his building. Right there, in the middle of the day, I got out of my car and cussed and hit him and yelled and swore that I would make sure I did everything in my power to hurt him the way he had hurt me. Neka finally managed to pull my ass back into the car and we drove away.

About six weeks after I pretty much humiliated myself in public, Eli tried reaching out to me with a call. A week later, when I hadn't responded, he called again and kept calling until I finally answered.

He told me he was sorry for how he had treated me. He said that he was no longer engaged and he wanted to be in my life, just as a friend. As much as I hated him and wanted no part of him in my life, I knew deep down inside that he and I had unfinished business. Every time I decided to cut my losses with Eli and move away from him, the universe would bombard me with everything about him. For example, after finding out about Eli's engagement, I knew I did not want him anywhere near me. I had made that decision not out of anger, but out of logic. I went to bed, and that night I dreamed of Eli begging me for food. I woke up in a panic; the dream was so intense and weird that it felt real. Later that morning on my way to work, I met a stranger on the train whose name was Elijah. Also, later that day I received a call from one of my co-workers whose wife had given birth that morning to a baby boy, whom they named Elijah. It was so fucking weird. I assumed this was God trying to get my attention and tell me that I had to allow Eli back in my life. I wasn't sure why, but I went with it.

I forgave him and agreed to be friends. He invited me to hang out, and the first time we met up we ended up spending the entire weekend together. The connection between us was even stronger than I remembered, but I also did not want to continue on without knowing what Eli and I were getting into. I wanted a commitment and I did not hesitate to bring that up. However, when I used the word "commitment," Eli would change the subject. He never told me he did not want a commitment with me, but he never he said he did either. This caused us to fight, which created a distance between us. During our times apart, he would go back to his fiancée. This cycle of garbage went on for almost five years.

❧ Chapter Six ❧

"If suffering brings wisdom, I would wish to be unwise."
William Butler Yeats

My anger towards Eli's decision to abandon me caused me more pain than I thought was possible for one person to feel, and I took my anger out on everyone; the customer service rep at my phone company, my co-workers, the barista at the local coffee shop, I mean everyone. I hated myself even more for opening my heart again, only for someone to shit all over me. I blamed myself for his behavior, because I allowed it. I thought that I was wrong to assume we had a spiritual connection, a divine love, and that I was just a stupid woman living in a fantasy. I felt like there was no such thing as soulmates or twin flames, only people using other people. Where was God in that? What was divine about it? Why are the loyal people always the ones who get hurt? Why do I pray and live my life as honestly as I humanly can, yet I am always the one suffering? Why was everyone – including God – turning their backs on me?

I would have these conversations with God all the time. I cried myself to sleep every single night. Yes, I was full of anger. Just when I thought I had hit rock bottom, little did I know things were about to get worse.

At 4:13 a.m. on an early Friday morning, I got a call I wish I had never had to receive in my lifetime. Neka had a night out and was heading home when she and her lover were hit by a drunk driver. When her mom called, I jumped out of my bed and rushed to the hospital. I did not even change out of my PJs or put on shoes. By the time I got to the hospital, Neka was dead.

I had fallen asleep that night crying over the fact that Eli had left me without even telling me he had moved on. I thought there was nothing more that could break my heart, but I was wrong. Losing my best friend, my soul sister, my ride or die, a woman who filled the void of not having a sister, was far worse.

When I entered the hospital room and saw her body lying there, I fell to my knees and wailed, screamed and cried until I lost my voice. I laid on the hospital floor, completely numb. I cried until there were no tears left to run down my face. My eyes were swollen shut and I could feel this heaviness in my chest; I thought I was having a heart attack. It hurt more than anything I could have imagined. It was surreal to think that I would never see or speak to my best friend again as long as I walked the earth in this body.

I can't remember how or when we left the hospital, but I do remember waking up in her bed at her mom's house and panicking. I went downstairs looking for Neka because this all had to be a dream. Where was my best friend? She's only 30 years old, she couldn't be dead. I needed to tell her about this nightmare. I screamed her name hoping she would respond.

I'm sorry, Amal, I don't mean to cry. It still feels like it just happened. I miss her every day, and I talk to her all the time. There are so many things I wish I could tell her and hear her response. I have never healed from losing her, and no one has ever replaced her place in my life. I loved that girl.

Her funeral was the worst day of my life. I did her eulogy and only God knows how I got through it.

Neka, my Neka...I found in you what I thought I would never experience in this life. I found a best friend, a soul sister, a kind-hearted, free-spirited being. A woman who smiled through the difficulties she faced and danced when life knocked her down. A woman who said she would never stop living, laughing, and loving, for those are the greatest gifts of life.

Neka, my Neka...You have taught me the definition of friendship and of love, of non-judgement towards another, and most importantly, you showed me what loyalty is. I will carry this gift you have given me all my life. I love you, I miss you, and I'll be talking to you when I sleep. Please come see me often.

Neka, my Neka, fly away butterfly, fly high.

I have never healed from losing her. They say time heals all wounds, but that's bullshit. I have hurt my whole life since the day Neka left this world, and there is not a day that goes by that I don't think of my best friend. I miss her. I imagine what she would have become? Would she had gotten married and had children, or would she had continued being the life of the party?

This was the darkest period of my life. I fell ill as the stress was too much. I took time off work to heal my body and my broken heart. I questioned God for allowing this to happen. I was angry at Him for letting my friend die, and for allowing Eli to come and ruin my perspective on love. I cried for months and lived in a constant state of despair. I was alone. No one understood my pain, so I kept it all to myself. I couldn't handle walking around in public, so I stayed in my apartment and only left when I needed a grocery store. I ate cup of noodles as I had no energy or desire for food. I took up smoking to calm my nerves, although I hated the taste. I dropped the menthols for vodka and hated that as well. I needed something to numb me, and whatever I choose to smoke or drink did not help.

My mom visited me often. I know she was worried that I had given up on life and on my dreams, but she never pushed me to get over it. Instead she sat silently with me until she had to leave. She did this for months. I appreciated her silent presence during this time, especially as I held a lot of resentment towards my parents. I felt like they never took my side; I was always the one wrong whenever I tried to defend myself against people who disrespected me. My mother sent me to live with a friend of hers one summer as her friend had kids around my age. It was supposed to be a fun summer break at their cabin, but my mom's friend mistreated me during this time. She acted like I was her servant; I cooked and cleaned for her family, and she would insult me saying things like my ass was too big, my hair was too nappy, and that her kids were better than me. I got home from that vacation and told my mom what had happened, yet my mom told me I was exaggerating and she continued to be friends with that bitch. I couldn't understand what mother would hear that her child was abused and not take their side. I carried this anger towards my parents, and especially my mother, for years. The rejection I felt from Eli only reminded me of the anger I held for my parents, and I hated Eli even more because he never reached out to me during this time. He knew Neka had died and he knew I would be devastated, but he never tried to contact me.

One Saturday afternoon, my mom asked me if I could visit her and dad as they were having some church folks over. As much as I had no desire to sit with my parents and their friends, I had spent the past five months in bed and my intuition wouldn't let me continue. When I arrived, I found out my mother had invited a pastor to bless the house as my cousin and her newborn were moving in.

Pastor Mason came and threw some holy water around. After the prayer ceremony, he asked to talk to me. I was annoyed that my mother had ambushed me with all this God talk, but Pastor Mason was polite so I sat with him in the dining room. He said something to me that I will remember for the rest of my life. He said, "I know you are angry and I know you question God for what has happened to Neka. But remember Malaika, *"God is still God."* It felt like a lightbulb had lit in my heart when he said those words.

I went home and stayed awake all night. I kept replaying in my mind what Pastor Mason had said, and I began to pray. The pain from losing Neka did not go away; in fact, it became worse as time went by. But I believed she was with her creator and that she was looking down on me and my every move. I had to make her proud. I had to follow my dreams since she never got a chance to follow hers. I had to live the life we both dreamed of. I had to go and travel the world and visit all the places we both talked about. I knew that if I carried her in my heart she would be right there with me, so that's what I did.

I took a longer leave of absence from work, sold my Mercedes and used the money – together with what I had saved up – to backpack around the world. I went to Shanghai first because that was on the top of Neka's bucket list. Being in Shanghai felt as if she was there with me; I swear sometimes I smelt her perfume as I was sight-seeing. When I left there, I backpacked through Europe. I went to Paris, Milan, and London before heading to Brussels to meet some family friends. I enjoyed visiting the landmarks, museums and cultural centers we had learned about in school. My last stop on my trip was to head to Miami and then back to Vancouver, but Eden, our family friend from Brussels, was heading to Zanzibar for a week with his friends and invited me to come. I had visited Africa before as my parents were both born there, but I had never been to Tanzania and this was on my bucket list. So, I changed my plans and off to Zanzibar we went.

We arrived at the resort after many hours of travel, and it was so beautiful. The water was a clear light blue and the sand was clean and white. The staff at the resort were friendly and the food was so tasty. I felt at peace for the first time since Neka passed. After dinner with Eden and his friends, I choose to walk by the ocean. It was like being in a dream. The breeze was warm, the water was clear and the smell of salt from the ocean calmed me. I walked the shores while the waves cleaned the sand off my feet, wishing Neka was there with me.

I stood facing the ocean when I felt someone touch my arm and said my name. I turned around and could not believe what I saw. It was Elijah!

Yes, he was once again back in my life; divine timing had brought us back together. I hadn't seen him in seven months, nor did I hear from him when Neka died. I wanted to feel anger and hate for him, but seeing his face that day brought back all the feelings I had for him. I loved him even more. I now believed that when two souls are meant to cross paths, everything else is irrelevant; the universe makes it happen even if they fight it.

Elijah said to me, "You are the last person I thought I would see here. I am so happy to see you. I've missed you Malaika, I've missed you so much. I wanted to reach out to you, but I was afraid that I would only cause you more anger. But I want you to know that every night I pray for you, and I pray that Neka is sitting with her creator at peace. I am so happy to see you."

๑๏ Chapter Seven ๏๑

"I'm so sorry; did my back hurt your knife?"
Unknown

Around this time, Amie had moved in with me temporarily as she lost her job and did not have a dime to her name. Mind you, her family lived in town, but when you're almost 40 moving back in with your mom and dad isn't exactly a first choice.

Over the years, Amie and I had grown to be close. She spent most of her free time at my house so moving in was not an issue. I introduced her to my family and friends and she fit right in. I told Amie all my dealings, hurts, and moments of happiness I had with Eli. She understood my pain as she too had a bad streak of useless men come in and out of her life. However, she had no clarity about who she was; she kept saying she wanted stability and to share her life with someone, but at the same time she kept dating married men. I did not want to judge her for it, because I knew she was insecure and would allow herself to be treated with the utmost disrespect. In a way, I felt sorry for her because I felt sorry for myself. I too was allowing Eli to disrespect me. So, I listened to her vent without telling her what I really thought of her home-wrecking ways; after all, who was I to judge when I was hoping a man who was engaged on-and-off to another woman would choose me instead. I felt as pathetic as I saw her to be.

I did tell her my truths, such as to stay away from men who were already in relationships or married, but it went in one ear and out the other. When these men used her and tossed her away, I felt nothing but pity for her.

During our friendship, however, she had her moments of jealousy. If I bought a pair of new shoes she would clearly feel some type of way, or when I got a promotion at work I could tell from her face and reaction that she begrudged my success. To a certain extent I understood her jealousy as she had no direction in life, although I did not appreciate it.

But as they say, when people show you who they are, believe them. Amie was about to show me who she really was.

After running into Eli in Zanzibar, we agreed to keep in touch. We called each other every couple of weeks to say hey. Although the communication between us was sporadic, that did not stop me from thinking of him all day every day. It had been like this since I met him. He was like a drug I couldn't let go of, even though I tried many times to do without.

Anyways, it had been about five months since I had seen Eli in Africa, and we were talking on the phone every now and then. I hated the fact that we both would just talk about the weather and how work was; basically having meaningless conversations. He would call and we both could feel that awkward energy; it was like we both had so much to say, yet neither of us had the courage to bring up the real issues. And since Eli was engaged, I needed to respect his choice and stay in my lane. Although I wasn't sure which lane that was. I wasn't fucking sure.

I vented all my frustrations to Amie, every detail of it, then one evening I got an enraged call from Eli. He said, "Malaika, seriously, you gonna send a friend of yours to test me? You know I'm fucking engaged." I wasn't sure what the hell he was talking about. I finally calmed him down and he tells me that he ran into a "friend" of mine who propositioned him. I was confused because the only friend Eli had ever met was Neka, and she was dead. Eli then explained the circumstances around his encounter with this "friend", and I realized it was none other than Amie.

I was livid to say the least. I went home packed all of Amie's things in trash bags – no pun intended – and waited for Amie to show up. When she did, I ripped her a new asshole and beat the living hell out of her. I told you, Amal, we have a lot more in common than you think. Back in my day I did not take shit from anyone, and since Amie thought she could put a knife in my back, I had to show her that I am not someone to fuck with. I threw that whore out of my house and never spoke to her again. I'm pretty sure she still lives with her parents to this day.

Amal, there will be wolves in sheep's clothing who will

befriend you during your lifetime. They come to teach you lessons of loyalty and betrayal. Now I'm not saying you need to go around beating up people; on the contrary, you should walk away because the people who seek to hurt you are already hurting. There is nothing you can do to cause them more pain than what they already face each day. They have their own path to walk and their own lessons to learn. Forgive them, and move on. If I had known this lesson then I would have never laid a hand on Amie, although I felt damn good after giving her a much-needed ass-whooping for thinking she could cross me and get away with it.

After this incident with Amie, I knew I needed to walk away from all the friendships that weren't serving me. I also better understood what jealousy entailed. People envy your looks, your kind-hearted nature, and how you handle life's difficulties without breaking a sweat. They envy you because what they thought would have broken you, didn't. They are jealous that you were born into a loving family, and that your siblings are your best friends. They can't stand to see you get back up and hold your head up high after life knocked you down. They envy your intelligence and the positive light in which you see yourself, and because you passed with excellence something that they couldn't get past. Jealousy isn't only geared towards material goods.

As I grew spiritually, I no longer related to most of the people I called friends because I didn't have any interest in meaningless friendships. People who showed signs of jealousy had to go, as did people who were more interested in my life than they were in theirs. The stage five clingers and negative Nancy's were all disposed of. I could no longer relate to people of a lower vibration. Neka was no longer physically with me, so I learned to be my own best friend. Eventually people who matched my vibration came into my life, and they have remained lifelong friends.

❧ Chapter Eight ❧

"I am in you and you in me, mutual in divine love."
William Blake

My belief in divine timing and relationships was back in my thoughts after seeing Elijah in Zanzibar. I was still unclear of what his role was to be in my life, but I trusted God eventhough it was painful knowing that he held another woman at night.

I also thought about past life relationships. As I mentioned before, I found it crazy that you can meet someone for the first time and just click with them while other people instantly rub you the wrong way. Is it a past life experience we are remembering, or is it just something in our souls that rejects certain people and accepts others? Did I have a soul contract with Jackson and Elijah? Is the concept of twin flames real?

It is said that a twin flame is someone who shares the same soul as you. They are you and you are them. They show you the shadow side of yourself as you show them theirs. The connection to a twin flame is so intense that it causes the less-awakened one to run, as they do not trust or understand why they feel such a strong emotional pull towards someone they barely know.

As I researched the concept of twin flames, I found it difficult to understand the concept of the other twin running. If Eli was indeed my twin, why was he denying a love that he so desired? I had no intentions of ever hurting him. All I wanted was to be with him and build a life with him, so why couldn't he see that we were meant for each other? I found out that twin flames can be separate in the physical third dimension, which is reality as we know it, but are never separated in the spiritual fifth dimension, which is where our higher selves can be found. When you are fulling your soul's purpose you are working in the fifth dimension, and I was convinced with everything inside of me that being with Eli was my soul's path to growth.

To this day, I'm not sure if I believe in the theory of twin flames. Perhaps I was just looking for answers at the time and this theory bounded me to my desire of wanting Eli to be with me. However, the synchronicities were out of this world. I would go places and see things that would remind me of him. A total stranger would come my way and start a friendly chat, and when they introduced themselves they would have Eli's name. I would hear songs on the radio that Eli loved. I would be alone at home and would smell his cologne. It was as if I could sense him around me, even when we went months without speaking or seeing each other. At night, while I laid in bed, I could hear Eli speak to me about his worries and pains; it's like we had a telepathic connection. At first I thought I was going insane, but whenever we reconnected he would tell me the same stories I heard him say to me telepathically. He would tell me that he "sensed" what was going on with me too. He could tell when I was angry and did not want anything to do with him. He could also tell when I softened my heart towards him, and that was his cue to contact me.

Once I was sitting at work and felt a shock, and immediately got a headache. I thought of Eli and hoped he was okay, though I am not sure why my mind ran to him. Later that evening Eli called me saying he was in a fender bender earlier that day; he was all right, but his car was totaled. This was when I began to think that perhaps we were connected in the fifth dimension, even though we had no physical contact for months at a time.

I also learned that twin flames only come together permanently in the third dimension when they both learn what they needed to about self-love; when they both have surrendered to the process and to God's will. Trust me, Amal, this is easier said than done, but I wanted to believe this was true. I knew with every ounce of my being that Eli and I had a spiritual connection, one that I would never find again in this lifetime. However, the process was so difficult. He kept coming in and out of my life, and every time he left I hated myself for letting him back in. I found myself living in "waiting" for him to come back.

I continued to research and question this idea of divine partnerships. There were times when I believed that Eli and I would eventually end up together – even though he was in a relationship with another woman – and there were even more times when I believed that I was a crazy bitch and needed to move on with my life. Here I was, a highly-educated woman, sitting around waiting on a man who has mistreated me to come back to me.

There were so many times when I was so hurt that he was away from me that I tried to explain our connection from a place of intellect to prove his actions. I wanted to stop hurting, and hating him would be easier than loving a man who wasn't there to love me back. No one understood my pain, and Neka was no longer around to support me through this.

I constantly questioned this idea of twin flames, but what I did know was that Eli would always be in my life in one form or another. Every time I tried to cut the connection by deleting his phone number or thinking of dating other men, the universe would give me signs and synchronicities that all pointed towards him. Every time I made the decision to cut him off, he would then come rushing back into my life as if he got a memo that said, "Malaika is walking away." When he returned it was frustrating, because I anticipated that he would only leave again.

I hated every part of this "twin flame" journey. I envied my friends and acquaintances who were getting married and having babies. All I wanted was to love and to be loved, but this desire eluded me at the time.

It's very painful, having a twin flame. Yes, the love felt between you both is so intense and pure and unconditional, but this type of relationship brings a lot of heartaches. It requires a lot of forgiveness and healing. You both must be on the same energetic level to guarantee no one will run from the connection. At the times that were the most difficult for me, I prayed that God had sent me a soulmate so I could cut my losses with Eli. I was willing to settle for a "lesser" relationship if it meant less pain.

While there were men who asked me out, and even some I went on dates with, there was never a second date because there was no connection to keep me attracted. I sat on these dates wishing I was sitting next to Eli instead.

During my many days of anger, my doubt in this theory would intensify. I would ask myself who the hell came up with this idea of "twin flames" anyway? I questioned the connection, and wondered if labelling Eli was limiting what I could have with him. Was I subconsciously putting this hardship out in the universe by naming Eli as my twin? Was he actually a twin flame or was he a soulmate, a life partner, a fucking user and manipulator, or just a bi-polar bitch-made man?

One morning my trainer Brandon asked me to brunch after our workout. Brandon was kind and very knowledgeable about fitness. He was also a good friend of mine and Neka's, and he was always with us during our party days. When we arrived at the restaurant I realized Eli was there with some buddies of his. I hadn't seen him in months, although we had talked on the phone during the previous week.

Eli looked angry when he saw Brandon and I walk in.

Before we sat down, we walked to his table to say hello. He was incredibly rude to both of us. I didn't understand why he was being so dismissive, but we smiled awkwardly and went to sit at our table. He gave us the dirtiest looks the entire time until he left. When I got home, Eli was waiting in front of my apartment building filled with anger. He said he felt "betrayed" that I did not tell him I was seeing another man. He screamed, "What the fuck were you doing with that man, Malaika?" I was so confused and angry at the audacity of this man who had left me so many times, fuming at the sight of me with another man. I let him talk out of his ass for a bit before I clarified that Brandon was a friend and my trainer. I instantly saw the relief in Eli's face when I told him the truth.

I invited him in and we talked for bit. Eli told me that he had broken up with his fiancée as she was cheating on him with a wealthy man. Her reasoning was that Eli was too focused on making money and building a solid foundation for them, and she felt neglected. He then expressed how sorry he was for the way he treated me. He regretted that due to his choices, I no longer saw him the same. I think at this point Eli wanted to know if I still loved him.

That night, after years since we first spent the night together, we made love. Eli left the next morning, but he shortly came back as he wanted to spend the day with me.

I was so happy when he returned, and it felt like when we had first met; we watched movies, talked, laughed and had a great time. Our visits continued for another week when Eli came by and told me that he needed to clear up some things so we were both on the same page. He came to tell me that he did not want a committed relationship as "titles change everything." He said they create expectations, and since he wasn't in the position to financially take care of me he did not want a committed relationship with me. I said nothing when he told me this, I simply asked him to leave. He tried to explain and ask me if he could stay, but I politely asked him again to leave.

When he walked out the door, I sat on the floor and cried, but this time my tears were for a different reason. These were tears of anger. This man was in the same fucking predicament since I met him. He needed to grow the fuck up and gain some fucking self-esteem. I cried because I couldn't believe the God I served and prayed to would allow this motherfucker back in my life to start this same shit all over again. I had done the fucking work on myself, I did not deserve this shit.

I was angry for all the years I kept a place in my heart for him. I was angry at all the lies I allowed him to tell. I was angry that I couldn't cut him loose; it was like he had a damn cord tied around my neck and I couldn't shake it off.

I knew then that despite how open and loving I was to Eli, he could only meet me as deeply as he met himself. And at that time, he did not love himself enough to love me. I finally got off the floor and opened the cabinet that held the remaining vodka I had purchased when Neka died. I chugged it and fell asleep. I woke the next morning hungover and headed into work. I was still so angry about what had happened the night before with Eli that I decided to send Eli a couriered letter to his office.

Dear Elijah Monroe, I would first like to say fuck you. I have had enough of your rejections, you dumb motherfucker with an English accent. You should be ashamed that your black ass is walking around here sounding like a fucking recording - (insert English Accent) "Press one if you want to speak to the operator." I am done with your bitch ass; I have no strength or desire to have you in my life any longer. You keep doing the same shit over and over. You keep apologizing, but your behavior has never changed. I am tired and since you don't want to make a commitment with me, I don't want one with you either — your broke ass don't deserve me. Do not contact me anymore.

Sincerely, Malaika.

P.S. Fuck you again, and oh, your dick game was shit last night.

The next day, I received a delivery from Eli; he sent me flowers at my office with a card that said, "I'm sorry, and you have every right to be angry. But we love each other and we need to be at least friends. Please, do not leave me Malaika."

Eli was emotionally manipulative, but I was aware of the manipulations. As much as I wanted to carry that anger towards him, this time I felt pity for him. He had no clue what this life was about. He focused on material things as he thought it would make him a "man." Don't get me wrong, it's in a man's nature to want to provide for his wife and his family, but he wasn't aware that he had to respect himself and learn that even without money, he is enough.

I also knew that he was heartbroken because of his fiancée cheating on him, and I felt sorry for what he was going through.

Months came and went and Eli's cycle of running and coming back continued, and I was tired of his shit. I tried to cut him loose; I even tried meditation and burning sage to rid myself of his energy. But nothing was working at all, and the more spiritual work I did the more I realized I needed to learn the lesson his presence was meant to teach me. Only then could I let him go with love. Being successful at letting love lead my way meant I had to let go of my ego's desire to hate him. I needed to forgive him, and I needed to pray for him. This was very, very difficult.

❧ Chapter 9 ❧

"Time can heal a broken heart, but it can also break a waiting one"
Unknown

I once saw an article in the newspaper written by a spiritual teacher named Angela who was also on this twin flame journey. In the article, she talked about the stages of a twin flame relationship. I attended her workshop when she visited Vancouver, and we quickly became friends and started to chat on the phone about our experiences. During one of our calls, she advised me to work on healing the wounds I carry from my past hurts; the ones I carry from the hurt my parents caused, from being betrayed by "friends," from losing Neka, and – most importantly – from my past relationships.

She advised me to do some "chakras clearing." I did not know what the fuck that was, but I was open to anything. I was so frustrated with Eli that if someone suggested that eating shit would make this pain in my heart disappear, I would have been open to it.

Angela held a healing clinic in her hometown of Phoenix, Arizona, and she invited me to attend one of them. A few weeks later, I was on a flight to Phoenix. The workshop was interesting; we did chakras clearing and I bought a bunch of stones and some more sage to cleanse my home. At the beginning of the healing clinic I thought I was a crazy person sitting with a bunch of other crazy people, doing some crazy ass shit with stones, sage, and meditating to weird music. But as the day continued, I couldn't help but think about what Neka would have thought of this experience. Truth is, if she was there in the physical, she would have been laughing so hard that we both would have probably gotten kicked out. These thoughts brought a smile to my face and opened my mind to the experience.

After the workshop, I invited Angela for dinner as I was curious to hear about where she was on her own journey and how she dealt with the pain of rejection. I guess I still needed someone to convince me that this twin flame theory was indeed real, and that I wasn't a crazy bitch stuck on a man who wanted nothing to do with me. Angela explained that the twin flame dynamic held a similar belief as that of the Red String of Fate. Per this myth, God tied a red string – red being the color of passion – around the ankles of those destined to be together in this life. This proverb, however, focuses on the fact that people are bound to each other rather than on finding their other half. There is a story that corroborates this red string of fate. It says that a little boy was walking home one night when he saw an old man reading a book. He asked the old man what he was reading, and the old man responded that it was a book on marriage. He told the young boy that he was destined to marry one girl. When he showed the little boy who the girl was, the boy did not like the idea as he did not want to get married. He then threw a rock at her and ran away as fast as he could. Years later, a marriage was arranged between the boy and the most beautiful girl in the village. When the boy unveiled his bride-to-be, he noticed she had a scar over her eyebrow. When he asked her about the scar, she told him that a little boy had thrown a rock at her as a child. This proved their fateful union.

At the core of this proverb is submitting to a higher power. Destiny will take its course and, in time, all will fall into place. It is important not to fight the red string, and when you find the person at the end of it you will need to have integrity, respect, devotion, unconditional love, empathy and loyalty to make this relationship reach its destined potential. The red string is there to remind lovers to remain faithful to each other. No matter how near or far away you are from this person, the thread remains that binds you two together. This thread is unbreakable; these two lovers are destined to be together.

After listening to Angela's take on this journey, I knew I needed to find a way to heal. I returned home and continued my healing process by going to church. I prayed, I read the bible, and I dug deep inside of myself. I learned who I was, I embraced all the good in me, and I became mindful of all my flaws. I stopped hating myself for letting others mistreat me. I forgave myself for making decisions that allowed me to hurt. I simply placed in my mind the intention to let go of the pain and anger, and soon after, my heart dropped the weight of the grudge I held towards myself, my parents, Jackson and Eli.

During my separation period from Eli, there was never a day I did not think of him. Trust me, I tried not to, but the more I tried, the more everything reminded me of him. I wondered what he was doing and what he ate that day, and I hoped he was happy. I still loved him, and when you love someone without conditions or expectations you wish them well, even when they choose to walk away from you. Loving him in spite of him being with someone else freed me from my pain. Eventually, I learned to detach from him and the outcome I desired.

As I let go of the Eli and Malaika saga, I began to feel at peace. Deep down, I always knew he would eventually contact me. I know it sounds crazy, but I couldn't shake the feeling that Eli and I had unfinished business. I continued to dismiss potential suitors. I did not want to have sex with anyone as I feared Eli would be hurt when he found out. I lived my life as if he was already with me, and I lived in this fantasy for a very long time. I think I was afraid that if I had sex with another man I would have subconsciously made the decision to leave Eli for good, and just the thought of leaving him brought tears to my eyes. I guess I wasn't ready to move on at this point, so I did everything I could to "wait" for him. Thinking about it now, I wouldn't have waited. I would have gone out and met other men and experienced the blessings of their friendship and perhaps even love. But the fear of opening my heart and getting hurt over and over again held me back, so I made excuses.

The more that time went by during our separation, the more I questioned Eli's purpose in my life. I questioned God again for allowing this man back in my life after I had let him go so many times. It's like I had no say in my own love life. I felt stuck and imprisoned, mostly by my own thoughts. I wanted to control the outcome; I wanted Eli with me NOW. Waiting for him seemed to bring back the pain I thought I had released.

The more I looked within, the more I realized that the blockages I felt were a result of my own thinking. I needed to surrender to the process. If Eli kept coming back in my life and leaving shortly after, I had to reflect on that treatment. I needed to find why it was that I expected him to leave as soon as he came back in. I realized that as much as I thought I had forgiven the past hurts, I was still holding on to the fear of getting hurt again. As a result, I was afraid of committing myself to the process, and Eli was only reflecting my fears back to me so I could heal them.

I went through what they call the dark night of the soul; I had to face everything I had buried deep inside of me. I cried sometimes for hours and days, and I wept every night for a very long time. My tears relieved me of all the negative energy I carried. I knew I needed to forgive my college sweetheart for not being man enough for me. I needed to apologize to him for dragging our relationship out for years, knowing very well I had no intentions of ever marrying him. I needed to forgive Jackson for destroying my belief in love. I needed to forgive Elijah for treating me like a doormat. But most importantly, I needed to forgive myself for beating myself up as I lived through life's toughest lessons.

There were many nights I stayed up until the sun came out, over-thinking choices I had made and how they lead to my own heart break. I found myself thinking about how much I hated who I was; not my physical look, but the circumstances I found myself in. I hated myself for loving so deeply, and I felt cursed by God for giving me the ability to love someone so completely and not having that love returned. I felt cursed for losing the one person who understood me, and who was no longer there for me to talk to and listen to. I hated myself for feeling so alone. I hated myself for feeling so unsupported. I hated the way I allowed someone else's treatment of me to make me feel so worthless. I hated myself, and I had fallen into a massive depression.

I worked through all these emotions and thoughts. As painful as they were, I knew this was how I needed to release the ache I carried in my bones, in every cell in my body, and especially inside my heart. No one would understand, and people would judge me if I told them what I was feeling and why I was feeling this way. So, I dealt with it alone. As part of my healing process I decided to cut off all contact with Eli. I wasn't sure if I had become strong enough to cut him off, or if I was just too tired and drained from fighting for someone who wasn't fighting back for me.

As I pulled away from Eli, he began to contact me

relentlessly. It was as if he could feel that I was not going to wait for him anymore, and that I was no longer willing and able to put up with his shit. I had no more patience for his confusion, and I simply could no longer afford to care. Caring had caused a lot of my pain, so my heart was closed to him and only him.

I prayed that God would take away my pain, and that He would show me the face of my husband who would be a better man than Eli could ever be. I prayed that God would relieve me of these lessons, as I had learned them. I prayed that God would have mercy on me.

At times during my healing, it was easy for me to blame Eli for my pain. After all, I was offering love to him while he rejected it. The pain of that rejection made me feel worthless, unwanted, used, and invisible. But the truth is, it was me who allowed him to walk back into my life every time he came back. It was me who had all the expectations for him to finally "see" me. I was the one who chose to see only the good in him, as opposed to the reality of how he treated me every time we would connect. I had my part to play in the whole situation, and it was time to take responsibility for my choices. I was so full of hurt that the only option I had now was to find a way to release it. I had to stare myself in the mirror and accept who I was. I had to watch myself cry and ache; I had to feel that pain since my stubbornness refused to "hear" Eli. Every time he mistreated me and I allowed him back in my life, that was my refusal to "hear" him. As the old African saying goes, if you can't hear, you can feel; because

I wasn't hearing Eli, I was feeling the pain that his actions caused.

I had to face these facts about myself in order to heal, and I chose to heal through prayer. As I learned to pray to find forgiveness within my heart, I also learned to be thankful for my experiences. I was grateful for the lessons I had learned as they helped me graduate to a higher level of my spirituality. I discovered what love was by learning what it was not. I found out that love and fear cannot coexist; you can jump in with all your heart and love fiercely or turn and run out of fear, but you certainly cannot do both.

I learned to stop getting angry at my family's wish for me to be married with kids by a certain age. I was okay with being the only one without a man at Christmas, even if it was "embarrassing" to my mother because I was the lonely one out of all my cousins.

One rainy Sunday afternoon I sat in my apartment drinking coffee and scrolling through pictures I had taken during my travels. I got a call from a number I did not recognize and chose to let my machine record a message. Then the same number called back; this time I picked up, and I wasn't expecting the voice at the end of that call. "Malaika," they said, "please don't hang up, this is Jackson."

Yes, Mr. Jackson had returned. I was so confused as to how he got my new number as I hadn't spoken to him since that day his mom told me about his affair. Why was he back in my life after all these years?

I told him I was shocked to hear from him. He responded by saying, "I'm sorry to bother you like this, but I've been looking for you for years and I just got your number. I wanted to see how you were doing. How have you been? Are you married? Do you have kids?"

This was the last person I wanted to talk to, and I wasn't ready to answer all his questions. I wasn't embarrassed that my answers were all no, I just didn't care to speak with him and I certainly did not care what Jackson thought of me. I said that it's been a long time and that he was acting like we were friends when we certainly weren't.

Jackson pleaded, "I know you hate me, and you have every right to, but I wanted to explain myself. I am not going to say that I know how you felt. However, I will tell you that I hated myself more than you could ever hate me. I hated myself for the fact that I knew you were hurting and that I was the cause of that hurt. I am so sorry. I ruined the best thing that ever happened to me, and I will regret hurting you for the rest of my life. I am hoping we could at least be friends."

I told him, "Look Jackson, it's been a long time. Yes, that was one of the most painful experiences I have had in my life, but I've moved on. I now know that you were placed in my path to teach me lessons about myself. I've learned those lessons and I thank you for that, but I have to go. I've got things to do right now."

I hung up the phone, still unsure as to why Jackson wanted to be in my life after all this time. The last time I had seen him was the day that we embraced and cried at the Chicago airport. Perhaps it was the universe testing me to see if I had truly forgiven him. Or, perhaps his presence was to remind me of the hurt in order to heal what was still lingering.

After that day, Jackson continued to call and leave messages asking if he could visit. I blocked his number, as well as several other numbers he would use to call me.

At that point it had been almost a year since I had cut Eli out of my life. I no longer had the energy to deal with his dysfunction. Time came and went; Christmas, Valentines, and Easter passed by. Eli would contact me during each holiday, hoping for a response that he never received.

One afternoon my mom and I went out to lunch and we ran into Eli. My mom didn't know much about what was happening between us, but she could see the sadness in both our eyes when we saw each other. She encouraged me to say hello, so I did. After that brief chat, we would see each other once in a while, and when we did meet it felt as though no time had passed at all. However, Eli wasn't ready; he told me once he wasn't sure if he was to "act" the way his family had raised him or like the version of himself he hides out of fear of judgement.

Every time Eli would go through his dark night of the soul, he would contact me. Somehow during our short calls, the dysfunction from his end started again. We would get into fights constantly, and I was beginning to believe that he only called to pick a fight. One time he called and started talking about wanting to purchase pillow cases, and he wasn't sure which brand or thread count would be best as shopping was a woman's thing. I suggested he got Egyptian cotton as those were what I bought, and oh help me lord, did he ever snap at me. He said, "I know you think you know everything, but I did not call you to ask for any fucking opinions about pillow cases. You need to know when not to talk." At first I would get mad and fight back with him, but soon I realized that whenever he called and started a fight he was hurting from the pain of betrayal he was experiencing in his own life. The anger he showed towards me was because he couldn't come to terms with me loving him when the whole world had turned their backs on him. He did not understand how I could still care for him, especially since he treated me like shit. He did not understand that I loved him unconditionally. No matter who he chose to be, I would still love him. Although I was no longer tolerating his abuse and meanness, I loved him. Just from a distance. I was too drained to go back and forth with him; I was too tired to even hear him out this time. For the second time, I stopped answering his calls and just let him be.

Shortly after I ran into a buddy of mine, Reuben, who I hadn't seen in years. Reuben was a tall, big-boned teddy bear who always had a huge, contagious smile on his face. However, this time he wasn't smiling. I asked him if he had time for a quick drink and he agreed.

We walked to a nearby restaurant and then I asked him to spill it as I could see that he was sad and hurt. He told me his girlfriend was cheating on him. I was shocked with how direct and honest he was, but I also knew that running into Reuben that day wasn't a coincidence. It was the universe's way of urging me to share my knowledge of healing with people who were hurting. I advised Reuben to feel what he needed to feel. Although society sometimes dictates that a man who cries is weak, vulnerability is actually healthy. I also advised him not to make any decisions regarding his girlfriend when he was emotional. I encouraged him to detach from his emotions before he decided if he could make the relationship work or if he needed to move on.

I left my meeting with Reuben feeling glad that I could help out a friend. I prayed for him on my walk home, asking that he finds the peace and love that he deserved.

As I continued to heal myself and learned to let go of Eli and the outcome of our saga, I turned my focus to my art. I loved photography and how a photo could tell a thousand stories. I wanted to show my life though pictures. I hoped to one day show the world love through the lens of my camera, and this is exactly what I did.

✄ Chapter 10 ✄

"Allow your passion to become your purpose and it will one day become your profession."

Gabrielle Bernstein.

I refocused my energy into taking more pictures. I loved seeing human interactions through my camera, so I travelled to different countries and experienced other cultures. The photos I took during my travels were amazing; there were stories being told in each picture. I met people who were very different from me, yet they all taught me that I was loved. They appreciated me as I was, which helped in my healing process.

Every time I came home from travelling, I would meet with Eli. He would tell me how great his career was going, how his wedding plans were on hold as his fiancée was still in school, how he was looking to buy a house, and so on. This was the same bullshit story he would tell me every time I saw him, and every time his eyes told me the truth. I saw how deeply sad he was. I knew he was hiding his pain behind this façade of "I'm making so much money so life is great." I tried inquiring what was really going on, but he would get defensive. So, I would drop the questions and pretend to care that he was house-hunting. At this point, he had been house-hunting for the last three years.

During our short visits, Eli would cunningly ask if I was seeing anyone. I would respond truthfully and I could see a sigh of relief in his face when I said no. But like always, our "reunion" wouldn't last. He would get angry at me for no reason and once again disappear from my life. During one of our many arguments, Eli screamed at me about my character. I wasn't sure if he knew me more than I knew myself, or if he didn't know me at all. Or, perhaps he was projecting his anger from the hurt he endured with his fiancée onto me. Either way, these conversations would replay in my mind over and over. I was hurt because the man I loved and desired did not respect me, but at the end of the day I didn't respect him either. I would also partake in name-calling, and in the dysfunction of our friendship. In hindsight, I now see that we both tried to hurt each other because it would make it easier to walk away. This was a testament to the fact that you cannot be "just friends" with someone you're in love with.

At this point of my journey, I no longer let his absence cause me pain. I would be sad that we were no longer communicating, but I was focused on my art. This had become my life's purpose and my relief from the pain of not being with Eli.

One afternoon I was at a print shop, enlarging a picture

I had taken in Turkey when I met Mrs. Joanne Johnson. She was a wealthy divorcée who also enjoyed photography. We got to talking and quickly became friends. She had been married and divorced four times already, and all of her exes were wealthy and well-established men. She had two adult kids who lived in Switzerland and rarely visited her.

She and I had an age gap between us, but we connected and she became the one person I could tell all my thoughts to without being judged. I called her Aunty JJ. She loved my pictures and encouraged me to chase my dreams. It was refreshing knowing that someone finally understood me and allowed me to be myself.

The more I refocused my energy, the more Eli contacted me. I still loved him deeply, but this time I had learned to detach from the outcome and allow whatever God had in store for me to play out. After all, what is mine will never elude me.

Even though I was making an effort to detach from him, I still obsessed over him and wondered if he missed me as much as I missed him. I wondered if he thought of me all day as I did of him. I hoped he loved me as much as I loved him.

Aunty JJ once asked me to visit her at her West Vancouver home. When I got there she was drinking wine as always – although this time, it was 10:00 a.m. – and there was an unfamiliar man there. She told me, "Malaika, my baby, you need to showcase your artwork. Your pictures bring me to life. The world needs to see your soul through the pictures you take and stories they tell. I want to give you a gift. This is Kairo, he's an event planner and he will help you find and book a location to showcase your work. Then we'll have a party!"

I instantly started crying. It had been my dream to showcase my art, and Aunty JJ was going to make it happen. When you choose to follow your life's path, you attract the people, places and things that help you achieve your dreams. Aunty JJ was sent by God to help me reach my goals. We set a date for the showcase for six months in the future and we immediately got to work. As the weeks went by, we found a location for the event and started advertising. Aunty JJ knew a lot of people in the city and she invited them all. This made me both excited and nervous at the same time.

I was happy to have something to focus on other than Eli, but I still missed him. I would hear about his accomplishments in his career through our mutual friends, and I was so proud of him. There were many times I wished I could pick up the phone and call him to say everything I had held in my heart. However, I respected the fact that he had another woman he chose to marry and I could not intervene. So instead, I would lay in bed and say out loud everything I wanted to tell him, hoping that he was indeed my twin and he could hear me or sense my excitement. I wanted to share what was happening in my life with him, but I couldn't at the time.

Kairo wanted me to accompany him at a wedding event to choose wines for my showcase. It was now only a month away and things were falling into place, but there was still a lot of work to do and the details had to be perfect because I was introducing my brand to the world. The event was jam-packed and every station had a lot of stuff to offer. While it was mostly wedding materials, this event was perfect as I was hosting a reception-style showcase. As we walked around looking at all the different options, I turned and locked eyes with Eli. He was there with his fiancée. This was the first time I had seen her in person. She was beautiful, and she was exactly like him – same accent, same culture, same everything – and I was just different. I wanted to run out of the event but my legs froze, so I grabbed Kairo's hand and told him we had to leave.

For the brief second Eli and I had locked eyes, I saw that he was embarrassed. Or, maybe he was scared that I would walk up to him and say something. A few days later he called me and I did not pick up, so he left a message saying he was sorry and that he wished I hadn't seen him at the wedding event. I did not respond to that message either. Perhaps I was jealous, or perhaps I was just mad at the fact that he thought seeing him would send me into an emotional turmoil. In truth, I ran because I was afraid of what I would say if I had spoken with them. I did not know if his fiancée knew of me and I wasn't trying to start any drama. He had made his choice and I respected it. Although the feelings I felt for him did not disappear, I also did not want to be a cause of any problems in his life.

I tried to get the image of them out of my mind, and I did so by focusing on my life's purpose: my photographs. My event was nearing and my to-do list kept me busy. This business left no room for me to feel any loneliness.

✒ Chapter 11 ✒

"It is in the giving of unconditional love that you make the other person realize what it is"

Unknown

The day of my showcase had arrived, and I was anxious yet grateful for what I had accomplished. Aunty JJ had invited all her wealthy friends, so the who's who of Vancouver were all supposed to be there. Knowing this made my stomach turn.

I started to get dressed, and thanks to Aunty JJ I had a team there to make me beautiful. She went above and beyond to make my day special, and I will love her forever for it. I wore a fitted red dress that showed the curves of my body. My hair was curled loosely and my makeup was done to perfection. I felt more beautiful that night than I had felt in my entire life. Before I left, I sat on my bed and looked up to the heavens and said, *Neka, please come with me tonight.*

I walked into the venue and all my dreams had been

fulfilled. I was officially a photographer – a great one at that – and that evening showed everyone who I was. I mingled with my guests and drank champagne, and all my showcased photos were sold by the end of the night.

As the evening continued, Aunty JJ pulled me aside and introduced me to a wealthy young investment banker. He was very cute, and he followed me as I mingled with my guests throughout the night. Eventually, he asked me to chat on the terrace outside. He was harsh flirting with me when I felt a tap on my shoulder, and I turned around to find Eli behind me.

I was shocked to see him at my event as we hadn't spoken in months. He glared at me and said he needed to speak with me. He grabbed my arm and pulled me towards him. I excused myself from my chat with the banker and went outside to Eli's car.

I said to him, "I wasn't expecting to see you here, I haven't heard from you in weeks. What are you doing here? Where do you get the audacity to pull me away from my own event?"

He responded, "I came because I am so proud of you. This is amazing. I always knew you could achieve what you put your mind to. Who is that man you were talking to?"

I instantly burst into tears and told Eli I needed to talk to him. I asked him not to interrupt me while I spoke. I said, "Eli, I'm happy to see you, and I'm so glad you came. But what has been going on between us is very difficult for me. I know what I feel for you is real, and I know that this feeling will last for as long as I live. This connection

81

between us is divine. Perhaps you don't believe in what I am saying, but from where I stand I can clearly see that this is true. However, you coming in and out of my life is no longer acceptable. I can't keep going like this. What do you want from me? I have no idea where we stand. You told me you did not want a relationship with me, and yet you come into my life seeking unconditional love, even just for one night. I've tried to remain friends, but the truth is that I cannot be friends with someone I am in love with. I am way too vulnerable to put myself in this position moving forward. I know our connection is strong, and it's scary, but you need to decide what you want from all this. You get all of me or none of me. I can't see you with another woman and still be 'friends' any longer. Look in your heart and tell me, what do you want?"

At this point I was crying, and Eli was as well. I could see that his walls were coming down as I spoke from my heart. I knew during our separation he was learning his own lessons, and that they were as difficult as mine. However, I was no longer going to be his rebound and keep allowing him to treat me like a toy for him to pick up and drop whenever he felt necessary.

Eli responded, "I know what you and I have is divine. I am aware of this. I am also afraid of it as I don't think I'm worthy of your love. I don't want to invest into you and not know if you will stay once you know who I really am. The connection I have with you scares me because I am afraid that once you know how deeply I love you, you will leave me like everyone else has. So instead I live in my mind, where I can be in love with you and your perfection without the risk of getting hurt."

I gave him an ultimatum. I told him, "I know with everything inside of me that this will work between us, but we both must work hard at it. I can't do it alone. You need to listen to your heart and choose. If you don't choose me, I will choose myself, and even though I will always love you, this will be the last time I will ever see or speak to you."

Eli then said, "The truth is I fucking love you, Malaika. I have loved you since the moment I laid eyes on you. I remember the dress you were wearing, the way you wore your hair and the smell of your perfume on that day we met five years ago. You changed me, and you changed my perception of what love is. You never asked me for anything, and you loved me even when I hurt you. My whole life people have made demands of me. I felt responsible for other people and that left no time for me to find out who I was and what I wanted. Until I met you. You made me think, and I did not want to think. You made me feel, and I did not want to feel. You made me see that life is beautiful. I have thought of you every day since the first day I met you. I lay in bed at night and I can feel your energy; sometimes I even smell your perfume. I hate that you confuse me. Seeing you talk to another man tonight felt like my heart with pierced with a knife. But, I've made my decision, and I am going back to my fiancée. She fits in with the vision I had for my life before you came and turned my whole world upside down, and the grass is green where you water it after all. I am going to marry her. So go, Malaika, and be with whomever you want to be with. I will never contact you again."

He left me once again, and for the first time I truly hated this connection. Twin flame, soul mate, karmic connection – whatever the hell this fucking was, I hated it and I no longer wanted any part of it. I had believed in my heart that someday Eli and I would be together, but after that conversation I lost all hope. I wanted to hate him enough to never respond to his calls ever again. I wanted to hate him enough to remember pain instead of love whenever he crossed my mind. I hated this connection, and I wanted to end it.

❧ Chapter 12 ❧

*"I understood what unconditional love was when I no
longer found it difficult to love myself FIRST."*
Ana Warner

I woke up the next morning with mixed feelings about the
night before. Eli had walked away again, and this time he
was gone for good. I was glad that he finally told me his
truth, and to some extent he had given me closure. But I
had no more tears, no more energy to try, and no more hope
with regards to Eli. I spent a lot of years looking for love
and feeling as though I was missing something. The truth
is, everything I wanted in love I already had in myself. I *am*
love. Once I realized that, I found this sense of worth and
empowerment that I did not think was possible. I realized
that what I wanted from Eli was to share the love I had
in myself with him, not to be codependent on him for the
love I felt I was missing. However, it was nice to get closure
from him and know that he felt what I knew I was feeling
all along. I guess in a sense I was lucky to get that closure

as most women don't. I was proud of who I was and what I had accomplished. I decided then and there, that I was going to start putting myself first.

I knew I had become a woman who was mature enough to be my man's emotional rock, to stand by his side, to soothe his pains and ease his worries. Any woman could look good and learn to cook and clean, but without the solid ground she provides for her man to safely vent his worries and cries to, she wouldn't be ready to be his wife.

And putting myself first started with me moving away from Vancouver. I had wanted to learn to speak French for as long as I could remember. My love for this language came when someone told me that in French people don't say "I miss you," they say "you are missing from me." Something about this made me fall in love with the language and so I decided to move to Montreal.

When I arrived, I started to live my life. I made new friends, I did my nails and hair all the time, I worked out, I ate healthy, and I took care of myself. I took myself out on dates to the movies, to art shows, and to concerts. I learned to love myself and appreciate my own company. The more love I showered myself with, the more I gravitated towards pleasant people. The friends I began to attract were on the same spiritual level as I was; they vibrated nothing but positivity. I could count on them, and they could count on me. I finally understood that all the trials I had been through in my life were lessons that lead me to this point. I finally loved myself. I embraced the good sides of me, and I was conscious of the flaws in my character. I worked on those flaws daily, but I never put myself down like I used to. I also stopped fantasizing about what it would be like to have Eli in my life. I let go, and let God guide me on my path.

I kept in contact with the banker I met at my showcase. Aunty JJ made sure he acted right towards me and I loved her for keeping him on his toes. About three months after I moved to Montreal, he decided to take our relationship to the next level so he moved to be with me. This was the first time I had been in a relationship since I was with Jackson, but who I was in this relationship was different. I was no longer depending on a man to be happy. I loved myself, first and foremost, which made it easy for me to love him. It was nice to have someone to spend Sundays with and to accompany me to dinner; someone to talk about life with. He was a very busy man and he travelled a lot for work, but he always made time for us. He was the full package. Although I loved him deeply, my heart didn't love him as much as it loved Eli. That being said, I was happy with him. He was stable, he was honest, he was a good provider, and he was kind. He was a good man.

I would think of Eli every day and had dreams of him while I slept, but I no longer longed to be with him; after all, for any relationship – even a twin flame one – to be in full permanent union, both parties had to surrender and choose the connection. I was the only one who chose to honor the connection, so I had to respect Eli's wishes and move on with my life. So, that is what I did.

My parents came to visit me in Montreal and my mom

mentioned that she had ran into Eli. He said he was finally getting married the following weekend at a "beautiful barn" outside of Vancouver. I should have been sad and hurt, but I wasn't. Instead I wondered who the fuck gets married at a barn. Don't they have cow shit laying around there? Eli was okay with smelling shit on his wedding day? Anyway, I wished him the best and I meant it.

The weekend after my parents returned to Vancouver, my banker proposed some much-needed alone time. After all, my mom is a handful and having her around for a week was exhausting. She was critical of how I decorated my home, the way I wore my hair, everything. As a treat, my banker had booked us into a swanky hotel for a night out in downtown Montreal. We went to dinner in a private room at the hotel's restaurant, which was filled with my favorite flowers and lit with candles. We had a very romantic dinner, and just before dessert was served my banker asked me to marry him. I was overjoyed, although I did find it ironic how the night Eli was getting married was the same night I got engaged to another man.

As we were finishing our dinner, my phone rang. I took the call as it was from my mother's number. I assumed my banker had told my parents his intentions before taking me to dinner that night, and since my mom said daily affirmations and fasted and prayed for "marriage to fall upon me" I thought this must be her calling out of excitement. When I answered, though, it wasn't my mother's voice on the phone. It was Eli's, and he was panicking.

When I heard his voice, I asked my banker to excuse me

as I needed to head to the washroom. I did not want my fiancé knowing it was motherfucking Eli on the line. I asked why the hell he was calling and if my parents were okay. He told me he had begged my mother to use her phone to call since he didn't have my new number. He said he needed to talk to me, and that he was heading to Montreal on the last flight. He begged me to meet him at the airport; told me his flight arrived at 5:35 a.m., and then he hung up.

I had no clue what had just happened. Somehow Eli had fucked up my engagement night by calling me, and that made me angry. I did not want my fiancé to sense that I was upset, so I politely continued with our evening. If he could read my thoughts, he would have known that I was raging inside. The thing is, while my fiancé was a good man, he did not pay attention to the details of my emotions. It was like he knew me but at the same time, he did not know me at all. Perhaps because I never showed him the parts of me that were scarred. I did not want to reopen the wounds that were still healing, so I only showed him the parts of me I was proud of. This is maybe why he couldn't see that the phone call had changed me.

In a single moment I had been sent back five years, and I was enraged that Eli was still holding on to me. Why was he calling me now? What did he want? Why was I his choice of solace when he was the one who abandoned me? Where was he when I needed him? He told me that the grass isn't greener on the other side, it's green where you water it; I guess now he's seen that he's been watering dead grass all along.

I couldn't sleep that entire night. Part of me wanted to meet him at the airport to hear him out – and cuss him out – while the other part wanted to not show up and shut that door forever.

When I finally fell asleep, I dreamed of Neka. She told me that what I needed was already mine, and all I had to do was receive it. I woke up and that dream felt so real, as if she was still alive. I did not know what she meant, whether she was encouraging me to go meet Eli at the airport or to shut him out for good. I wasn't sure if he was coming back into my life to mess things up and leave like he did for the last five years, or if he was finally ready to apologize for the hurt he had caused me. Sometimes it's too late to make things right. I said a prayer and asked God to guide my steps.

In the end, I decided to meet Eli at the airport and hear him out. I'm sure you want to know what he said to me; Well, Amal, you can go ask him yourself. Grandpa Jo's full name is Joseph Elijah Monroe, my time flame, soulmate, life partner, and best friend; my Eli.

TO BE CONTINUED

To be continued...

Interested in hearing Eli's side of the story and how he won Malaika back? Follow my Instagram account for announcements on when part 2 of this story will be launched. Instagram: anico28

Author Biography

Ana-Maria Warner, was born in Bucharest, Romania to a Romanian Mother and Liberian Father. Ana was raised during her early years in West Africa and soon immigrated to Canada as a teenager. She studied at the University of Saskatchewan where she received a Bachelor of Sciences. But Ana's heart has always been with the art of writing. At age 11, Ana started writing poetry, short stories and lyrics to music. Her favorite topic to write about was (and still is) love. As she grew older, her quest to understand who people are and why they behave the way they do lead her to educate herself on Astrology. This is where she stumbled upon the concepts of twin flames, soul mates and karmic relationships. She researched these concepts for the past seven years while closely studying the experiences she encountered in her own love life. And in late 2016 she started writing Malaika's story. Although this story is fiction, it is certainly relatable to everyone who has once had their heart broken.